Illustrations by Janice St. Marie

# Quick Dishes

## FOR THE WOMAN IN A HURRY

*Culinary Arts Institute* ®

ISBN: 0-8326-0631-6

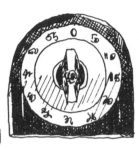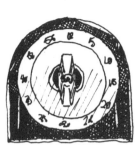

## Contents

# Quick Dishes

This cookbook has been written for the working woman, busy with career and apartment; the homemaker whose day is filled with community, club, home and family activities; the hostess whose guests sometimes arrive without notice.

Here are 332 recipes, any of which can be prepared in 30 minutes or less. The timing indicated is merely a guide, since everyone works at a different speed.

From these recipes can be planned attractive, complete meals from appetizer to dessert; or simple main dish-and-salad meals.

Save time by careful menu planning and shopping. Make the most of electric blenders, pressure saucepans, canned and frozen foods and shelf-ready mixes. Use spare time to prepare some food in advance.

Let these time-saving methods and recipes guide the way to better, faster meals.

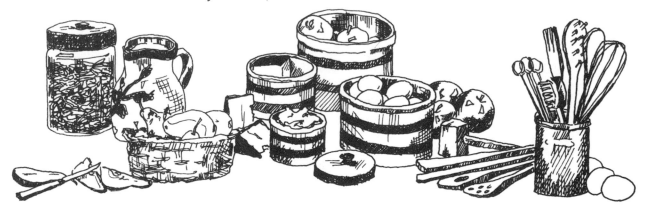

# It's Smart to be Careful

**There's No Substitute for Accuracy**
Read recipe carefully.

Assemble all ingredients and utensils.

Select pans of proper kind and size. Measure inside, from rim to rim.

Use standard measuring cups and spoons. Use measuring cups with subdivisions marked on sides for liquids. Use graduated nested measuring cups for dry or solid ingredients.

Check liquid measurements at *eye level*.

Level dry or solid measurements with straight-edged knife or spatula.

Sift (before measuring) regular all-purpose flour, or not, in accord with the miller's directions on the package. When using the instant type all-purpose flour, follow package directions and recipes. Level flour in cup with straight-edged knife or spatula. Spoon, without sifting, whole-grain types of flour into measuring cup.

Preheat oven at required temperature.

Beat whole eggs until thick and piled softly when recipe calls for well-beaten eggs.

Beat egg whites as follows: *Frothy*—entire mass forms bubbles; *Rounded peaks*—peaks turn over slightly when beater is slowly lifted upright; *Stiff peaks*—peaks remain standing when beater is slowly lifted upright.

Beat egg yolks until thick and lemon colored when recipe calls for well-beaten egg yolks.

Place oven rack so top of product will be almost at center of oven. Stagger pans so no pan is directly over another and they do not touch each other or walls of oven. Arrange single pan so that center of product is as near center of oven as possible.

**For These Recipes—What To Use**
**Baking Powder**—double-action type.
**Bread Crumbs**—two slices fresh bread equal about 1 cup soft bread crumbs or cubes. One slice dry or toasted bread equals about ½ cup dry cubes or ¼ cup fine, dry crumbs.

**Buttered Crumbs**—soft or dry bread or cracker crumbs tossed in melted butter or margarine. Use 1 to 2 tablespoons butter or margarine for 1 cup soft crumbs and 2 to 4 tablespoons butter or margarine for 1 cup dry crumbs.

**Chocolate**—unsweetened chocolate. A general substitution for 1 sq. (1 oz.) chocolate is 3 to 4 tablespoons cocoa plus 1 tablespoon shortening.

**Chocolate (no melt)**—1 oz. packets or envelopes chocolate-flavored product or ingredient.

**Cornstarch**—thickening agent having double the thickening power of flour.

**Cream**—light, table or coffee cream containing 18% to 20% butterfat.

**Heavy or Whipping Cream**—containing not less than 30% butterfat.

**Flour**—regular all-purpose flour. When substituting for cake flour, use 1 cup minus 2 tablespoons all-purpose flour for 1 cup cake flour.

**Grated Peel**—whole citrus fruit peel finely grated through colored part only.

**Herbs and Spices**—ground unless recipe specifies otherwise.

**Oil**—salad, cooking. Use olive oil only when recipe states.

**Rotary Beater**—hand-operated (Dover type) beater, or use electric mixer.

**Shortening**—a hydrogenated vegetable shortening, all-purpose shortening, butter or margarine. Use lard or oil when specified.

**Sour Milk**—cold sweet milk added to 1 tablespoon vinegar or lemon juice in a measuring cup to fill to 1-cup line; stir. Or use buttermilk.

**Sugar**—granulated (beet or cane).

**Vinegar**—cider vinegar. Use other vinegars when specified.

**How To Do It**
**Baste**—spoon liquid (or use baster) over cooking

food to add moisture and flavor.

**Boil**—cook in liquid in which bubbles rise continually and break on the surface. Boiling water at sea level is 212°F.

**Clean Celery**—trim roots and cut off leaves. Leaves may be used for added flavor in soups and stuffings; inner leaves may be left on stalk when serving as relish. Separate stalks, remove belmishes and wash. Then proceed as directed in recipe.

**Clean Garlic**—separate into cloves and remove outer (thin, papery) skin.

**Clean Green Pepper**—rinse and slice away from pod and stem; trim off any white membrane; rinse away seeds; cut into strips, dice or prepare as directed in recipe.

**Clean and Slice Mushrooms**—wipe with a clean, damp cloth and cut off tips of stems; slice lengthwise through stems and caps.

**Clean Onions (dry)**—cut off root end and a thin slice from stem end; peel and rinse. Prepare as directed in recipe.

**Cut Dried Fruit (uncooked) or Marshmallows**—cut with scissors dipped frequently in water.

**Dice**—cut into small cubes.

**Flake Fish**—with a fork separate canned (cooked) fish into flakes (thin, layer-like pieces). Remove bony tissue from crab meat; salmon bones are edible.

**Flute Pastry Edge**—press index finger on edge of pastry, then pinch pastry with thumb and index finger of other hand. Lift fingers and repeat procedure to flute around entire edge.

**Fold**—use flexible spatula and slip it down side of bowl to bottom. Turn bowl quarter turn. Lift spatula through mixture along side of bowl with blade parallel to surface. Turn spatula over to fold lifted mixture across material on surface. Cut down and under; turn bowl and repeat procedure until material seems blended. With every fourth stroke, bring spatula up through center.

**Marinate**—allow food to stand in liquid (usually an oil and acid mixture) to impart additional flavor.

**Measure Brown Sugar**—pack firmly into measuring cup so that sugar will hold shape of cup when turned out.

**Measure Granulated Brown Sugar**—see substitution table on package before pouring into measuring cup.

**Melt Chocolate**—unsweetened, over simmering water; sweet or semi-sweet, over hot (not simmering) water.

**Mince**—cut or chop into small, fine pieces.

**Prepare Double-Strength Coffee Beverage**—prepare coffee in usual manner (method and grind of coffee depending upon type of coffee maker) using 4 measuring tablespoons coffee per ¾ standard measuring cup of water.

**Prepare Quick Coffee**—for one cup coffee beverage, place one teaspoon concentrated soluble coffee (instant) into cup. Add boiling water and stir until coffee is completely dissolved. For 1 cup of double-strength coffee beverage, increase concentrated soluble coffee to 1 tablespoon.

**Prepare Quick Broth**—dissolve in 1 cup hot water 1 chicken bouillon cube for chicken broth, or 1 beef bouillon cube or ½ teaspoon concentrated meat extract for meat broth.

**Rice**—force through ricer, sieve or food mill.

**Scald Milk**—heat in top of double boiler over simmering water or in a heavy saucepan over direct heat just until a thin film appears.

**Sieve**—force through coarse sieve or food mill.

**Simmer**—cook in liquid just below boiling point; bubbles form slowly and break below surface.

## Oven Temperatures

| | |
|---|---|
| **Very Slow** | 250°F to 275°F |
| **Slow** | 300°F to 325°F |
| **Moderate** | 350°F to 375°F |
| **Hot** | 400°F to 425°F |
| **Very Hot** | 450°F to 475°F |
| **Extremely Hot** | 500°F to 525°F |

Use portable oven thermometer to double check oven temperature.

## When You Deep Fry

A deep-frying thermometer is an accurate guide for deep-frying temperatures.

If a thermometer is not available, the following bread cube method may be used as a guide. A 1-in. cube of bread browns in:

**60 seconds at** . . . . . . . . . . . . . . . . . . . . 375°F

When using an automatic deep fryer, follow manufacturer's directions for amount of fat and timing.

## When You Cook Syrups

A candy thermometer is an accurate guide to correct stage of cooking. Put the thermometer into syrup mixture after sugar is dissolved and boiling starts. A 3-inch depth of syrup is advisable to take an accurate thermometer reading; if necessary, tip pan to obtain this depth. If thermometer is cold, heat it in warm water before plunging it into the hot syrup.

## When You Broil

Set temperature control of range at Broil. Distance from top of food to source of heat determines the intensity of heat upon food.

# How To Cook Vegetables

Wash fresh vegetables, but do not soak them in water for any length of time.

**Baking**—Bake such vegetables as potatoes, tomatoes and squash without removing skins. Pare vegetables for oven dishes, following directions given with recipes.

**Boiling**—Have water boiling rapidly before adding vegetables. Add salt at beginning of cooking period (¼ teaspoon per cup of water). After adding vegetables, again bring water to boiling as quickly as possible. If more water is needed, add boiling water. Boil at a moderate rate and cook vegetables until just tender.

In general, cook vegetables in a covered pan, in the smallest amount of water possible and in the shortest possible time. Exceptions for amounts of water or for covering are:

**Asparagus**—arranged in tied bundles with stalks standing in bottom of a double boiler containing water to cover lower half of spears—cover with inverted double boiler top.

**Broccoli**—trimmed of leaves and bottoms of stalks. If stalks are over 1-in. in diameter, make lengthwise gashes through them almost to flowerets. Cook quickly in a covered skillet or saucepan in 1 in. of boiling, salted water 10 to 15 min., or just until tender.

**Cabbage (mature)**—cooked, loosely covered, in just enough water to cover. Cabbage (young) cooked, tightly covered, in a minimum amount of water (do not overcook).

To restore color to red cabbage, add a small amount of vinegar at end of cooking period, just before draining.

**Cauliflower (whole head)**—cooked, uncovered, in a 1 in. depth of boiling, salted water for 5 min., then covered, 15 to 20 min.

**Mature Root Vegetables (potatoes, rutabagas, parsnips)**—cooked, covered, in just enough boiling, salted water to cover vegetables.

**Spinach**—cooked, covered, with only the water which clings to leaves after final washing.

A desirable boiled vegetable is free from excess water, retains its orginal color and is well seasoned. Pieces are uniform and attractive.

**Broiling**—Follow directions with specific recipes.

**Frying and Deep Frying**—Follow directions with specific recipes.

**Panning**—Finely shred or slice vegetables. Cook slowly until just tender in a small amount of fat, in a covered, heavy pan. Occasionally move with spoon to prevent sticking and burning.

**Steaming**—Cooking in a pressure saucepan is a form of steaming. Follow directions given with saucepan because overcooking may occur in a matter of seconds.

*Note:* Some saucepans having tight-fitting covers may lend themselves to steaming vegetables in as little as 1 teaspoon water, no water or a small amount of butter, margarine or shortening.

**Canned Vegetables**—Reduce liquid from can to one-half of original amount by boiling rapidly. Add vegetables; heat thoroughly and quickly.

**Home-Canned Vegetables**—Boil 10 min. (not required for tomatoes and sauerkraut).

**Dried (dehydrated) Vegetables**—Soak and cook as directed in specific recipes.

**Frozen Vegetables**—Do not thaw before cooking (thaw corn on cob and partially thaw spinach). Break frozen block apart with fork during cooking. Use as little boiling salted water as possible for cooking. Follow directions on package.

# APPETIZERS

**Hors d'Oeuvres**

*For a Relish Tray*—Pass several of the following: **crab apples,** spiced; **olives; radishes; carrot sticks; cheese-stuffed celery;** salted **nuts; sharp cheese** wedges; canned **shoestring potatoes; prunes** stuffed with seasoned **cream cheese.**

*Cheese Popcorn*—Sprinkle ½ cup (2 oz.) grated **cheese** and salt over 1 qt. hot **popped corn.**

*On Wooden Picks*—Arrange on picks and insert in an apple, orange, grapefruit or firm cheese base, combinations of the following: **beet cubes;** canned **mushrooms** or **pineapple chunks** marinated in **French Dressing** (page 56); **gherkins; pearl onions; cocktail sausages;** cubed canned **luncheon meat** or **frankfurter pieces** dipped in **Peppy Cocktail Sauce** (see Fish Cocktails, page 14); or seasoned **cream cheese** balls rolled in chopped **nuts** or minced **dried beef.**

**Canapes**

*Canapes are appetizers consisting of small savory bits of seasoned foods spread on a base. Variety can be gained by using different kinds of bread and cutting the slices into interesting shapes. Use brown bread, rye, wheat or pumpernickel bread, plain or toasted. Or use melba toast, small rolls, crackers or potato chips for canape bases.*

*Pastry Canapes*—Roll out pastry (page 75) and cut into small strips or shapes. Sprinkle strips or shapes with grated **cheese.** If desired, sprinkle **poppy seeds** or **caraway seeds** over grated cheese. Place on baking sheet and bake at 425°F 10 to 15 min., or until lightly browned.

*Quick Spreads*—Spread on canape bases prepared **cheese** or **sandwich spreads,** or soften **liver sausage** with **cream** and season with grated **onion,** mixing well before spreading onto bread.

*Appetizer Cheese Dip*—Put into electric blender container in order ¼ cup **sour cream,** 2 tablespoons **pineapple juice,** 1 pkg. (3 oz.) **cream cheese,** ¼ lb. **Blue cheese,** 3 sprigs **parsley,** 1 **onion slice,** 1 clove **garlic,** 4 or 5 drops **Tabasco.** Blend the mixture until smooth.

*Canape Wedges*—Carefully trim bottom crust from a large round loaf of **pumpernickel bread.** Cut 3 slices, each about ½ in. thick, from loaf and use as layers. Spread 2 layers with **process cheese food spread.** Put slices together, spread-side up. Top with third layer. Blend 1 can (3 oz.) **deviled ham** with 1 or 2 tablespoons **ketchup.** Mix thoroughly before spreading. Spread mixture over third layer. Top with wedge-shape slices **cheese.** Chill in refrigerator until serving time. Following outline of cheese wedges, cut loaf into wedge-shape servings.

*Sardine Canapes*—Cream ¼ cup **butter** or **margarine** until softened; blend in 1½ teaspoons **lemon juice** and 1½ teaspoons **prepared mustard.** Spread **toast strips** with butter mixture. Top each strip with one chilled **sardine,** well drained. Garnish with a thin strip of **pimiento.**

**Cocktails**

*Vegetable Juices*—Season chilled **tomato juice** with **celery leaves, onion, salt, pepper, lemon** juice, **Worcestershire sauce** or **Tabasco.**

Mix 2 parts **clam juice** with 1 part **tomato juice;** season and garnish with **lemon.**

Serve **vegetable juice** combinations chilled or hot, topped with **Sweetened Whipped Cream,** (page 66).

*Fruit Juices*—Serve one or more fruit juices such as **apricot, cranberry, orange, pineapple** or **grapefruit.** Mix with equal amounts of **ginger ale,** if desired. Serve in juice glasses with cracked ice and **mint** sprigs, **maraschino cherries, orange** or **lemon** slices.

Serve hot juices such as **apple cider** with **cinnamon stick** stirrers.

*Fruit*—Choose colorful combinations of fresh, canned or thawed frozen **fruits.** Top with **fruit sherbet.**

*Fish*—On **lettuce** in cocktail glasses, serve **Cooked Shrimp** (page 36), or drained contents of two 5-oz. cans **shrimp.**

Top with **Peppy Cocktail Sauce**—Combine 1 cup **ketchup,** 1 tablespoon each of **sugar, prepared horse-radish** and **lemon juice,** 1 teaspoon **Worcestershire sauce,** 1 teaspoon **onion juice,** ½ teaspoon **salt** and a few drops **Tabasco.**

*Note:* **Crab meat** (two 6½-oz. cans), bony tissue removed, may be substituted for shrimp.

# Chili con Queso Dip

| 1 | cup chopped onion |
| 2 | cans (4 ounces each) green chilies, chopped and drained |
| 2 | large cloves garlic, mashed |
| 2 | tablespoons cooking oil |
| 1 | pound process sharp Cheddar cheese, cut into chunks |
| 1 | teaspoon Worcestershire sauce |
| ¼ | teaspoon paprika |
| ¼ | teaspoon salt |
| ½ | cup tomato juice |

1. Saute onion, green chilies, and garlic in oil in cooking pan of chafing dish over medium heat until onion is tender.
2. Reduce heat to low, and add remaining ingredients, except tomato juice. Cook, stirring constantly, until cheese is melted.
3. Add tomato juice gradually until dip is the desired consistency. Place over hot water to keep warm.
4. Serve with **corn chips.**

*3¼ cups dip*
*25 min.*

# SOUPS

## Potato-Leek Soup

3   **cups water**
3   **medium-size (about 1 lb.) potatoes (about 2½ cups, diced)**
¼   **cup (2 or 3) thinly sliced leeks (white part only)**
1   **teaspoon salt**
⅛   **teaspoon pepper**
3   **slices bacon**
½   **cup cream**
½   **cup milk**
2   **tablespoons chopped parsley**
1   **tablespoon butter or margarine**

1. Bring water to boiling in a 2-qt. saucepan having a tight-fitting cover.
2. Meanwhile, wash, pare and dice potatoes.
3. Add potatoes to boiling water with leeks, salt and pepper.
4. Cover saucepan and simmer gently about 15 min., or until potatoes are tender.
5. Meanwhile, dice and panbroil (see Calf's Liver with Bacon, page 32) bacon.
6. Remove saucepan from heat and drain vegetables, reserving the broth. Force vegetables through food mill, ricer or sieve into broth.
7. Blend in bacon and cream, milk, parsley, and margarine.
8. Reheat soup and serve hot.

*6 servings*
*30 min.*

**Vichyssoise:** Follow recipe for Potato-Leek Soup. Substitute for the water, 3 cups **Quick Chicken Broth** (three times recipe, page 10). Increase potatoes to 6 (about 2 lbs.). Cook potatoes with leeks, seasonings and ½ cup (about 1 medium-size) chopped **onion** and ⅓ cup finely chopped **celery.**

When potatoes are tender, put vegetables through food mill and mix into the broth. Cool. Pour into a 2-qt. screw-top jar. Cover jar tightly and store in refrigerator.

To serve, pour well-chilled mixture into a bowl and blend in 2 cups chilled **cream.** Serve soup cold, sprinkled with chopped **chives.**

*Note:* This mixture, without 2 cups cream, will keep 1 to 2 weeks in refrigerator if stored in a tightly covered jar. Prepare a day or two before serving so that Vichyssoise can reach the table as fast as the chilled soup and cream can be mixed.

*30 min.*

# Blender Pea Soup

1   pkg. (10 oz.) frozen peas
2   cups milk
1   tablespoon all-purpose flour
2   tablespoons butter or margarine
½   teaspoon salt
½   teaspoon nutmeg
⅛   teaspoon pepper
1   small onion, quartered
    Chopped parsley

1. Set out a 1½-qt. saucepan.
2. (Cover electric blender container before operating to avoid splashing.)
3. Break apart frozen peas with a fork and set aside.
4. Set out milk.
5. Put into blender container in order, 1 cup of the milk and flour, butter or margarine, salt, nutmeg, pepper and onion.
6. Cover, turn on motor and blend. Continue to blend while gradually adding one-half of peas. Use rubber spatula to scrape down sides of container so that ingredients will become evenly mixed. Blend until contents of container are thoroughly mixed, about 1 to 1½ min. Empty contents of container into saucepan.
7. Pour second cup of milk into container. Blend while gradually adding remaining peas. Stir contents of container into mixture in saucepan. Bring to boiling, stirring occasionally.
8. Serve immediately, topped with parsley.

*4 servings*
*20 min.*

**Main Dish Soup:** Follow recipe for Blender Pea Soup. Increase milk to 2½ cups; divide equally for two additions. Gradually add 1 cup cubed, cooked **ham** with last addition of peas. Sliced **frankfurters** added just before heating, may be substituted for ham.

*20 min.*

# Jiffy Lobster Bisque

1     6½-oz. can lobster meat (about 1 cup, drained)
1½    cups milk
1¼    cups (10½- to 11-oz. can) condensed cream of mushroom soup
1¼    cups (10½- to 11-oz. can) condensed tomato soup
1     teaspoon Worcestershire sauce
5     drops Tabasco
      Few grains cayenne pepper
1     tablespoon sherry extract

1. Set out a 2-qt. saucepan.
2. Drain canned lobster meat and break into small pieces.
3. Set lobster aside.
4. Combine milk and mushroom in the saucepan over medium heat.
5. Blend in tomato soup, Worcestershire sauce, Tabasco, and cayenne pepper.
6. Add lobster and bring mixture to boiling.
7. Remove from heat and stir in sherry extract.
8. Serve at once.

*5 servings*
*20 min.*

# Rich Oyster Stew

| | |
|---|---|
| 2 | cups milk |
| 2 | cups cream |
| 1 | pt. oysters |
| ¼ | cup butter or margarine |
| 2 | teaspoons salt |
| ⅛ | teaspoon pepper |

1. Set out a 2-qt. saucepan.
2. Scald milk and cream.
3. Meanwhile, drain oysters reserving liquid.
4. Pick over oysters to remove any shell particles.
5. Melt butter or margarine in the saucepan.
6. Add oysters with reserved liquid. Simmer 3 min., or until oysters are plump and edges begin to curl. Stir oyster mixture into scalded milk with salt and pepper.
7. Serve at once with oyster crackers.

*6 servings*
*25 min.*

Chile con Queso Dip 14

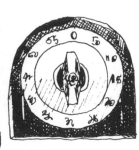

# BREADS

## Bread In Many Ways

*Croutons—* Melt 2 to 3 tablespoons **butter** or **margarine** in a large, heavy skillet over low heat. Meanwhile, if desired, trim crusts from 2 slices toasted **bread.** Cut bread into ¼ to ½-in. cubes. Put cubes into the skillet and toss until all sides are coated and browned.

*About 1½ cups Croutons*

*Toast Cups—* Remove crust from 6 slices **bread.** Lightly brush both sides of slices with melted **butter** or **margarine.** Gently press each slice into a muffin pan well to form a shell.

Bake at 350°F 12 to 15 min., or until lightly browned. If desired for a dessert, fill with sweetened **fruits.** Serve immediately.

*6 Toast Cups*

*French Toast Sandwiches—* Blend together ⅓ cup (3 oz. can) **deviled ham,** ¼ cup finely chopped **celery,** 2 tablespoons **cream,** ½ teaspoon **Worcestershire sauce** and ¼ teaspoon **dry mustard.**

Spread mixture on 4 slices **bread** and top with 4 more slices. Carefully dip sandwiches, one at a time, into a mixture of 3 **eggs,** slightly beaten, ⅔ cup **milk** or **cream,** 1 tablespoon **sugar** and ½ teaspoon **salt.** Coat each side well and place in hot skillet containing 3 tablespoons hot **fat.** Brown at one time only as many sandwiches as will fit easily into the skillet. Turn once with spatula. If necessary, add more fat to keep sandwiches from sticking.

For sandwich topping, melt 3 tablespoons **sugar** in a heavy skillet over low heat. Add 4 slices (9-oz. can, drained) **pineapple** and brown lightly on both sides. Place on sandwiches. Cut sandwiches diagonally and serve hot.

*4 servings*

*French Toast—* Follow recipe for French Toast Sandwiches; omit ham filling. Do not form sandwiches; dip and fry single bread slices; omit pineapple. Serve toast with **butter** or **margarine** and **maple syrup; confectioners' sugar; tart jelly;** or **Link Sausages** (page 32).

*Quick Cheese Bread—* Make diagonal cuts almost through 1 small loaf unsliced **bread.** Arrange in cuts, slices of **American cheese.** Place loaf in a greased shallow baking dish.

Brush a mixture of ⅓ cup melted **butter** or **margarine,** 1½ teaspoons **caraway seeds** and 1 teaspoon **dry mustard** over top and sides.

Bake at 350°F 15 to 20 min., or until bread is lightly browned and cheese is melted.

Meanwhile, heat in a small skillet 2 tablespoons **butter** or **margarine** with about ¼ cup finely chopped **anchovies,** 1 tablespoon **lemon juice** and few drops **Tabasco.** Pour over bread just before serving.

*8 servings*

*Garlic Bread—* Make diagonal cuts about ½ in. apart, almost through to bottom of 1 loaf **French bread.** Put ⅓ cup **butter** or **margarine** in a small skillet with 1 clove **garlic,** crushed (in garlic press or in mortar with pestle). Heat until butter or margarine is melted. Brush over bread and in cuts. Sprinkle with **paprika,** grated **cheese** or **poppy seeds,** if desired. Place loaf on baking sheet.

Bake at 350°F 10 to 15 min., or until bread is heated thoroughly. Serve hot.

*1 loaf Garlic Bread*

*Coffee Cake Loaf*—Trim crusts from 1 loaf unsliced **bread.** Cut bread into halves lengthwise. Cut each half into 6 squares, cutting almost through bread. Place on greased baking sheet, uncut surface down. Brush tops, sides and cuts with ¼ cup melted **butter** or **margarine.**

Cut with pastry blender or two knives, 2 tablespoons **butter** or **margarine** into a mixture of ½ cup firmly packed **brown sugar,** 3 tablespoons flour and 2 teaspoons **cinnamon** until mixture resembles coarse cornmeal. Sprinkle over tops of bread.

Bake at 400°F 12 to 15 min., or until bread is lightly toasted. To serve, place the halves together to resemble the original loaf.

*6 servings*

*Quick Coconut Coffee Bread*—Trim crusts from 1 loaf unsliced **bread.** Cut diagonally into wedge shapes, cutting almost through bread. Place on lightly greased baking sheet, uncut surface down. Brush top and sides with **sweetened condensed milk.** Sprinkle top and sides with about ½ cup **flaked coconut** and ¼ cup (about 1 oz.) chopped **nuts.**

Bake at 350°F about 20 min., or until bread is lightly browned.

*6 servings*

*Tomato-Cheese Sandwiches*—For each sandwich, panbroil (see Calf's Liver with Bacon, page 32) 2 slices **bacon** until transparent. Trim crusts from slice of bread and toast on one side. Spread untoasted side with 1 tablespoon **mayonnaise.** Top with 1 slice **tomato,** peeled, 1 slice process **American cheese** and panbroiled bacon slices. Arrange on broiler rack.

Set temperature control of range at Broil. Place rack under broiler with top of sandwich 3 in. from heat source. Broil about 4 min., or until cheese is melted. Serve immediately.

*Cheese Rusks*—Top **rusks** with **mayonnaise, cheese** and **bacon** as sugested in Tomato-Cheese Sandwiches. Broil until cheese is melted.

*Orange Quickies*—Combine 3 tablespoons **sugar,** 2 tablespoons **orange juice concentrate,** undiluted, and 1 tablespoon **butter** or **margarine** in a small saucepan. Cook until sugar is dissolved, stirring constantly. Stir in ⅓ cup **flaked coconut** and spoon glaze over brown-and-serve rolls. Bake according to directions on package.

*Enough glaze for 2 doz. rolls*

*Maple Toast*—Set temperature control of range at Broil. Remove crusts from slices of **bread.** Put onto baking sheet and place in broiler about 3 to 5 in. from source of heat. Toast until golden brown. Turn and brush with **butter** or **margarine.** Sprinkle generously with soft **maple sugar.** Broil until sugar is melted. Sprinkle with coarsely chopped **walnuts** or **pecans.** Serve hot.

# Tender-Rich Buttermilk Biscuits

| | |
|---|---|
| **2** cups sifted all-purpose flour | 1. Set out a baking sheet. |
| **1½** teaspoons baking powder | 2. Sift flour, baking powder, salt, and baking soda together into a bowl. |
| **1** teaspoon salt | 3. Cut lard in with a pastry blender or two knives until mixture resembles coarse corn meal. |
| **½** teaspoon baking soda | |
| **⅓** cup lard | |
| **¾** cup buttermilk | |
| Milk | |

4. Make a well in the center of the dry ingredients. Pour buttermilk in all at one time.
5. Stir with a fork until dough follows fork. Gently form dough into a ball and put on a lightly floured surface. Knead lightly with finger tips 10 to 15 times.
6. Gently roll dough to ½-in. thickness. Cut with a floured cutter or knife, using an even pressure to keep sides of biscuits straight. Place biscuits on baking sheet, close together for soft-sided biscuits, or 1 in. apart for crusty sides.
7. Lightly brush tops with milk.
8. Bake at 450°F 10 to 15 min., or until biscuits are golden brown.

*About 2 doz. 1½-in biscuits*
*30 min.*

**Tender-Rich Rolled Biscuits:** Follow recipe for Tender-Rich Buttermilk Biscuits. Omit the baking soda, increase the baking powder to 2 teaspoons and substitute ¾ cup **milk** for buttermilk.

*30 min.*

**Tender-Rich Drop Biscuits:** Follow recipe for Tender-Rich Buttermilk Biscuits or recipe for Tender-Rich Rolled Biscuits. Increase buttermilk or milk to 1 cup. Omit kneading, rolling and cutting. Drop by spoonfuls onto baking sheet.

*25 min.*

**Bacon Biscuit Sandwiches:** Panbroil (see Calf's Liver with Bacon, page 32) 3 slices **bacon.** Cut each slice into 4 pieces and set bacon aside. Follow recipe for Tender-Rich Buttermilk Biscuits or recipe for Tender-Rich Rolled Biscuits. Roll dough ¼ in. thick. Cut dough with floured cutter and brush biscuit tops lightly with **egg,** slightly beaten. Place one-half of biscuits on baking sheet. Press a piece of bacon on top of each and sprinkle with ½ teaspoon grated **Cheddar** or **Parmesan cheese.** Place remaining biscuits on cheese, egg-side down. Gently press together and bake as in Tender-Rich Buttermilk Biscuits recipe.

*30 min.*

**Tender-Rich Rolled Shortcakes:** Follow recipe for Tender-Rich Buttermilk Biscuits or recipe for Tender-Rich Rolled Biscuits. Sift 2 tablespoons **sugar** with dry ingredients. Cut dough with floured knife or 3-in. cutter. Or cut dough into halves and roll each portion to fit an 8-in. round layer cake pan. Spread one-half of rounds, or one large round, with melted **butter** or **margarine.** Top with remaining rounds or round. Place on baking sheet or in layer cake pan and bake as in Tender-Rich Buttermilk Biscuits recipe.

*To Serve*—Split shortcakes and spoon one-half of **Sweetened Crushed Berries** (page 69) over the bottom halves. Replace tops and spoon over remaining berries and top with **Sweetened Whipped Cream** (page 66).

*30 min.*

**Tender-Rich Drop Shortcakes:** Follow recipe for Tender-Rich Buttermilk Biscuits. Sift 2 tablespoons **sugar** with dry ingredients. Increase milk or buttermilk to 1 cup. Omit kneading, rolling and cutting. Drop by heaping tablespoonfuls onto baking sheet. Serve as suggested in Tender-Rich Rolled Shortcakes.

*25 min.*

**Cinnamon or Apple Rolls:** Follow recipe for Tender-Rich Buttermilk Biscuits. Grease baking sheet. Roll dough into rectangle about ¼ in. thick. Brush dough with 2 tablespoons melted **butter** or **margarine.** Sprinkle with a mixture of ¼ cup firmly packed **brown sugar,** ¼ cup (about 1 oz.) finely chopped **nuts** and 1 teaspoon **cinnamon.**

Or, spread dough with a mixture of 1½ cups (about 2 medium size) finely chopped **apples,** ½ cup **sugar** and 1 teaspoon **cin-**

**namon.**
Beginning with long side, roll and press edges together to seal. Cut into 1-in. slices. Do not brush tops with milk. Place flat on baking sheet and bake.

*30 min.*

### Orange Rolls:
Follow recipe for Tender-Rich Buttermilk Biscuits. Grease baking sheet. Roll dough into rectangle about ¼ in. thick. Brush with 2 tablespoons **butter** or **margarine.** Reserving 1 tablespoon grated peel, sprinkle dough with mixture of ½ cup **sugar** and ¼ cup grated **orange peel.** Beginning with long side, roll and press edges together. Cut into 1-in. slices. Do not brush tops with milk. Place flat on baking sheet and bake at 425°F about 15 min.
*Prepare Orange Glaze*—Combine in a saucepan, ½ cup **sugar,** ¼ cup **light corn syrup,** 2 tablespoons hot **water** and reserved orange peel. Bring to boiling and cook 2 min., stirring once or twice. Set aside to cool until rolls are removed from oven. Spoon Orange Glaze over tops of rolls and serve.

*30 min.*

### Coconut Twists:
Follow recipe for Tender-Rich Buttermilk Biscuits or recipe for Tender-Rich Rolled Biscuits. Grease baking sheet. Roll dough into rectangle about ¼ in. thick. Brush dough with 2 tablespoons melted **butter** or **margarine.** Sprinkle lightly with ⅔ cup firmly packed **brown sugar** and 1 cup **flaked coconut.** Cut dough into 5x1-in. strips. Fold strips in half and twist. Do not brush tops with milk. Place on baking sheet and bake about 8 min.

*30 min.*

# Muffins

| | |
|---|---|
| ¼ | **cup butter or margarine** |
| 2 | **cups sifted all-purpose flour** |
| ⅓ | **cup sugar** |
| 1 | **tablespoon baking powder** |
| ½ | **teaspoon salt** |
| 1 | **egg, well beaten** |
| 1 | **cup milk** |

1. Grease bottoms of 12 2½-in. muffin pan wells.
2. Melt butter or margarine and set aside to cool.
3. Sift flour, sugar, baking powder and salt together into a bowl.
4. Make a well in the center of dry ingredients and set aside.
5. Blend egg and milk thoroughly.
6. Blend in melted shortening. Add all at one time to dry ingredients. With not more than 25 strokes, quickly and lightly stir until dry ingredients are barely moistened. The batter will be lumpy and break from spoon. (Too much mixing will result in muffin tunnels.)
7. Cut against side of bowl with spoon to get enough batter at one time to fill each muffin pan well two-thirds full. Place spoon in well and push batter off with another spoon or spatula. Fill any empty wells one-half full with water before placing pans in oven.
8. Bake at 425°F 20 to 25 min., or until muffins are an even golden brown.
9. Run spatula around each muffin and lift out. If necessary to keep muffins warm before serving, loosen muffins and tip slightly in wells. Keep in a warm place.

*1 doz. Muffins*
*30 min.*

**Cranberry Muffins:** Follow recipe for Muffins. Wash and drain 1 cup **cranberries**; chop coarsely. Mix with 3 tablespoons **sugar**. Blend with sifted dry ingredients.

*30 min.*

**Blueberry Muffins:** Follow recipe for Muffins. Rinse and drain 1 cup fresh **blueberries.** Gently fold blueberries into batter with final strokes.

*30 min.*

**Double-Top Muffins:** Follow recipe for Muffins. Place a cooked, dried **apricot** half in bottom of each greased muffin pan well. Spoon batter into wells. Top batter with a crumbly mixture of ½ cup firmly packed **brown sugar,** ½ cup **butter** or **margarine,** softened, ⅓ cup sifted **flour** and 1 teaspoon **cinnamon.**

*30 min.*

# Blitzkuchen

| | |
|---|---|
| ⅓ | **cup (about 1 oz.) chopped walnuts** |
| ⅓ | **cup sugar** |
| 1½ | **teaspoons cinnamon** |
| 1 | **tablespoon butter or margarine, melted** |
| 1 | **cup sifted all-purpose flour** |
| ½ | **cup sugr** |
| 1½ | **teaspoons baking powder** |
| ½ | **teaspoon salt** |
| ¼ | **cup shortening** |
| 1 | **egg, well beaten** |
| ½ | **cup milk** |

1. Grease bottom of an 8-in. round layer cake pan.
2. *For Topping*—Mix thoroughly in order and set aside walnuts, ⅓ cup sugar, cinnamon, and butter or margarine.
3. *For Cake*—Sift together flour, ½ cup sugar, baking powder and salt.
4. Cut in shortening with pastry blender or 2 knives until pieces are size of rice kernels.
5. Make a well in center of dry ingredients and add egg and milk all at one time.
6. Stir, mixing only enough to moisten dry ingredients, about 15 strokes. Turn batter into pan and spread evenly to edges. Sprinkle topping over surface and gently pat down with back of a spoon or fork.
7. Bake at 375°F about 20 min., or until a wooden pick or cake tester comes out clean when inserted gently in center of coffee cake.
8. Serve Blitzkuchen hot.

*6 servings*
*30 min.*

**Orange Kuchen:** Follow recipe for Blitzkuchen. Substitute grated **orange peel** for cinnamon in topping. For cake, decrease milk to ⅓ cup and add 3 tablespoons **orange juice.**

*30 min.*

**Caraway or Poppy Seed Kuchen:** Follow recipe for Blitzkuchen. Omit topping. Mix in 2 teaspoons **caraway** or **poppy seeds** with sifted dry ingredients. Before baking, sprinkle 2 tablespoons **sugar** evenly over the batter.

*30 min.*

**Crunchy Kuchen:** Follow recipe for Blitzkuchen. For topping, substitute **brown sugar** for granulated sugar, ½ cup coarsely crushed **cereal flakes** for nuts and increase butter or margarine to 2 tablespoons.

*30 min.*

# Corn Bread Squares

5 tablespoons shortening
1 cup sifted all-purpose flour
¼ cup sugar
1 tablespoon baking powder
¾ teaspoon salt
1 cup yellow corn meal
1 egg, well beaten
1 cup milk

1. Grease bottom of an 8x8x2-in. pan.
2. Melt shortening and set aside to cool.
3. Sift flour, sugar, baking powder, and salt together into a bowl.
4. Mix in corn meal.
5. Make a well in center of dry ingredients and set aside.
6. Blend egg, milk and shortening thoroughly.
7. Add all at one time to dry ingredients. Beat with a rotary beater until just smooth, being careful not to overmix. Turn into pan and spread to corners.
8. Bake at 425°F about 20 min., or until a wooden pick or cake tester inserted in center of bread comes out clean.
9. Cut into squares and serve.

*9 servings*
*30 min.*

**Crisp Corn Sticks:** Follow recipe for Corn Bread Squares. Spoon batter into 12 hot, greased corn stick pan sections filling each three-fourths full. Bake at 425°F 10 to 15 min.

*25 min.*

# Buttermilk Waffles

½   **cup butter or margarine**
2   **cups sifted all-purpose flour**
1   **tablespoon sugar**
2   **teaspoons baking powder**
1   **teaspoon baking soda**
½   **teaspoon salt**
3   **egg yolks**
2   **cups buttermilk**
3   **egg whites**

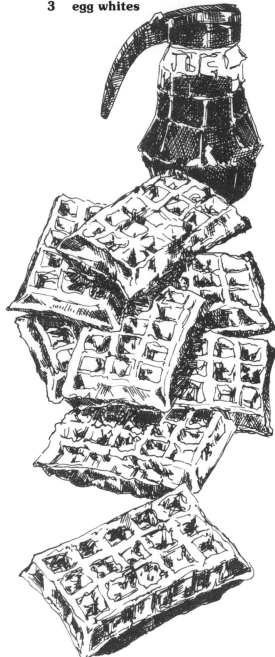

1. Heat waffle baker while preparing waffle batter.
2. Melt butter or margarine and set aside to cool.
3. Sift flour, sugar, baking powder, baking soda, and salt together into a large bowl and set aside.
4. Beat 3 egg yolks until thick and lemon colored.
5. Add gradually the melted butter or margarine and buttermilk.
6. Continue to beat until well blended. Add liquid mixture all at one time to dry ingredients; mix only until batter is smooth.
7. Beat 3 egg whites until rounded peaks are formed.
8. Spread the beaten egg whites over the batter and gently fold together.
9. Unless temperature is automatically shown on waffle baker, test heat by dropping a few drops water on baker. It is hot enough for baking when drops of water "sputter" on surface. Pour batter into center of waffle baker. It's wise to experiment to find out the exact amount of batter your waffle baker will hold; use that same measurement (spoonfuls or cupfuls) in future waffle baking.
10. Lower cover and allow waffle to bake according to manufacturer's directions, or until steaming stops (4 to 5 min.). Do not raise cover during baking period. Lift cover and loosen waffle with a fork.
11. Serve immediately with butter or margarine and warm maple syrup.

*About 8 servings*
*30 min.*

**Sweet Milk Waffles:** Follow recipe for Buttermilk Waffles. Omit baking soda and increase baking powder to 1 tablespoon. Substitute **milk** for buttermilk.

*30 min.*

**Cheese Waffles:** Follow recipe for Buttermilk Waffles. Fold ½ cup (2 oz.) grated **Cheddar cheese** into batter after folding in beaten egg whites.

*30 min.*

**Chocolate Drop Waffles:** Follow recipe for Buttermilk Waffles. Sprinkle about ¼ cup **semi-sweet chocolate pieces** over batter before closing waffle baker.

*30 min.*

**Poppy Seed Waffles:** Follow recipe for Buttermilk Waffles. Add ¼ cup **poppy seeds** to a skillet with the butter or margarine; melt butter or margarine, stirring occasionally.

*30 min.*

**Spice Waffles:** Follow recipe for Buttermilk Waffles. Sift 1 teaspoon **cinnamon** and ½ teaspoon **nutmeg** with dry ingredients. Add 3 tablespoons **molasses** with liquid ingredients.

*30 min.*

**Main Dish Waffles:** Follow recipe for Buttermilk Waffles. Sprinkle 2 tablespoons shredded cooked **ham** over batter before closing waffle baker. Or, serve a **creamed vegetable, meat, fish** or **poultry** mixture on waffles.

*30 min.*

**Dessert Waffles:** Follow recipe for Buttermilk Waffles. Serve waffles immediately with **ice cream** and any of the suggested **Toppers for Ice Cream** (page 68).
*For Shortcake*—Spoon **Sweetened Crushed Berries** (page 69) or sweetened **fresh peach slices** over waffle. Spread **Sweetened Whipped Cream** (page 66) over fruit. Top with another waffle and layer of fruit and whipped cream. Sprinkle with **nutmeg.** If using frozen fruit, thaw partially.

*30 min.*

# Griddlecakes

|   |   |
|---|---|
| 2 | tablespoons butter or margarine |
| 1½ | cups sifted all-purpose flour |
| 1½ | teaspoons baking powder |
| ½ | teaspoon salt |
| 2 | egg yolks |
| 1⅓ | cups milk |
| 2 | egg whites |

1. Set a griddle or heavy skillet over low heat.
2. Melt butter or margarine and set aside to cool.
3. Sift flour, baking powder, and salt together into a bowl.
4. Make a well in center of dry ingredients and set aside.
5. Beat egg yolks and milk together.
6. Add all at one time to dry ingredients. Beat with rotary beater until well blended and smooth. Blend in melted butter or margarine.
7. Set aside while beating egg whites.
8. Using a clean rotary beater, beat egg whites until rounded peaks are formed.
9. Spread beaten egg whites over the batter and gently fold together.
10. Test griddle or skillet; it is hot enough for baking when drops of water, sprinkled on surface, dance in small beads. Lightly grease griddle or skillet if manufacturer so directs. Pour batter from a pitcher or large spoon into small pools about 4 in. in diameter, leaving at least 1 in. between. Turn griddlecakes as they become puffy and full of bubbles. Turn only once.
11. Serve immediately with warm maple syrup.

*About 12 Griddlecakes*
*30 min.*

**Cherryland Griddlecakes:** Follow recipe for Griddlecakes. Fold 2 cups rinsed, stemmed and pitted ripe, red, **tart cherries** into batter after folding in beaten egg whites.

*30 min.*

**Blueberry Griddlecakes:** Follow recipe for Griddlecakes. Rinse and drain 2 cups fresh **blueberries.** Fold blueberries into batter after folding in beaten egg whites. Serve with honey or butter.

*30 min.*

**Banana Griddlecakes:** Follow recipe for Griddlecakes. Peel and dice 2 **bananas** with brown-flecked peel. Fold into batter after folding in beaten egg whites.

*30 min.*

**Polka Dot Griddlecakes:** Follow recipe for Griddlecakes. Fold 1 pkg. (6 oz.) **semi-sweet chocolate pieces** into batter after folding in beaten egg whites.

*30 min.*

# MAIN DISHES

## Broiled Beef Steaks

**Beef steaks, such as porterhouse, T-bone, sirloin or club, cut about 1 in. thick**
**1 teaspoon salt**
**¼ teaspoon pepper**

1. Set out beef steaks. Allow about ½ lb. meat per serving.
2. Set temperature control of range at Broil.
3. Arrange beef steaks on broiler rack. Place in broiler with top of steak 2 in. from heat source; broil 8 to 10 min. on each side. (The short cooking time for rare steaks; the longer cooking time for medium-done steaks.)
4. Meanwhile, for each pound of meat, mix salt and pepper.
5. When steaks are browned on one side, sprinkle with one-half of seasoning mixture. Turn and broil second side. Test for doneness by cutting a slit along the bone and noting color of meat. Season second side of meat.

*Note:* For 2-in. steaks, broil with tops of steaks 3 in. from heat source, allowing 15 to 20 min. on each side.

*20 min.*

**Broiled Lamb Chops:** Follow recipe for Broiled Beef Steaks. Substitute shoulder, rib or loin **lamb chops** for beef steaks. Broil about 5 to 7 min. on each side. Garnish with **tomato** and **water cress.**

*15 min.*

**Broiled Ham Slice:** Follow recipe for Broiled Beef Steaks. Substitute ¾- to 1-in. thick **ham slice** for beef. Omit seasoning mixture. Broil about 8 to 10 min. on each side. Serve with **Mustard Sauce** (page 59).

*20 min.*

# Beef Patties

1 ½   lbs. ground beef
⅓   cup (1 slice) fine, dry
     bread crumbs
¼   cup grated onion
1 ½   teaspoons Worcestershire
     sauce
1 ½   teaspoons salt
¼   teaspoon pepper
2   medium-size apples (about
     1 ½ cups, shredded)
2   tablespoons fat

1. Set out a large, heavy skillet.
2. Combine ground beef, bread crumbs, onion, and Worcester-shire sauce and a mixture of salt and pepper, and mix lightly.
3. Wash, quarter, core, pare and shred apples.
4. Mix lightly and thoroughly with meat. Shape into 6 patties, about ¾ in. thick.
5. Heat fat in skillet.
6. Add patties and brown both sides over medium heat, turning occasionally. Allow 10 to 15 min. for cooking. Drain off any excess fat as it accumulates.

*6 servings*
*30 min.*

**Fork-Tender Steak:** Follow recipe for Beef Patties. Omit shredded apple. Add 1 **egg** well beaten, with bread crumbs and seasonings. Place meat mixture on broiler rack and pat into a large oval about 1½ in. thick.
Set temperature control of range at Broil.
Place broiler rack in broiler with top of meat 3 in. from source of heat; broil 12 to 15 min. When browned on one side, carefully turn and broil 8 to 10 min. on second side. Serve with panbroiled **bacon** (see Calf's Liver with Bacon, page 32).

*30 min.*

**Bacon Wrapped Beef Patties:** Follow recipe for Fork-Tender Steak. Shape meat mixture into 6 patties. Wrap 1 slice **bacon** around each patty and secure with a wooden pick. Broil, allowing about 10 min. on first side and 8 min. on second side.

*30 min.*

**Apricot Lamb Patties:** Cut 4 slices **bacon** in ¼-in. pieces and pan broil (see Calf's Liver with Bacon, page 32) until crisp.
Meanwhile, follow recipe for Beef Patties. Omit shredded apple. Substitute **ground lamb** for ground beef. Add 1 **egg,** well beaten, with bread crumbs and seasonings. Divide mixture into 6 portions.
Stuff 6 large, cooked **apricot halves** with bacon pieces. Place an apricot half on each meat portion; gently shape patty around apricot. Cook as in Beef Patties recipe. Garnish lamb patties with sprigs of **mint.**

*30 min.*

# Baked Ham Slice

| | |
|---|---|
| 1 | smoked ham slice, cut about ½ in. thick |
| | Whole cloves |
| 2 | tablespoons brown sugar |
| 2 | tablespoons fine, dry bread crumbs |
| 1 | teaspoon grated orange peel |
| ½ | teaspoon dry mustard |
| 1 | orange |
| | Maraschino cherries, cut in rings |
| ¾ | cup orange juice |

1. Place ham slice in an 11¾x7½x1¾-in. baking dish.
2. Allow ⅓ to ½ lb. meat per serving.
3. Insert whole cloves into ham slice at 1-in. intervals.
4. Sprinkle over ham a mixture of brown sugar, bread crumbs, orange peel, and dry mustard.
5. Rinse orange and cut into ¼-in. slices.
6. Arrange slices on ham over sugar mixture. Garnish with maraschino cherries.
7. Carefully pour orange juice over top of ham slice.
8. Bake at 300°F about 30 min. Remove cloves from ham slice before serving.

*30 min.*

**Pineapple Baked Ham Slice:** Follow recipe for Baked Ham Slice. Substitute **lemon peel** for orange peel, canned **pineapple juice** for orange juice and 3 canned **pineapple slices** for the orange slices.

*30 min.*

**Ginger Baked Ham Slice:** Follow recipe for Baked Ham Slice. Substitute **lemon peel** for orange peel and **ginger ale** for orange juice. Omit orange and cherry garnish.

*30 min.*

**Plum Baked Ham Slice:** Follow recipe for Baked Ham Slice. Substitute **syrup** drained from 1 17-oz. can **purple plums** for orange juice. Arrange plums around ham slice. Omit orange and cherry garnish.

*30 min.*

# Sweet-Sour Meat Balls

| | |
|---|---|
| 1 | 12-oz. can luncheon meat |
| ⅔ | cup uncooked rolled oats |
| 2 | tablespoons all-purpose flour |
| ¼ | cup milk |
| 1 | egg, well beaten |
| 1½ | tablespoons prepared mustard |
| 1 | teaspoon Worcestershire sauce |
| 1 | tablespoon butter or margarine |
| ⅓ | cup firmly packed brown sugar |
| 1 | tablespoon all-purpose flour |
| ½ | cup water |
| ¼ | cup vinegar |
| 1 | tablespoon light corn syrup |
| 6 | whole cloves |

1. Set out a heavy skillet.
2. Grind contents of luncheon meat.
3. Mix thoroughly with oats, 2 tablespoons all-purpose flour, milk, egg, mustard, and Worcestershire sauce.
4. Shape into 6 balls.
5. Heat butter or margarine in the skillet.
6. Add balls and brown over medium heat, turning occasionally.
7. Meanwhile, prepare Sweet-Sour Sauce. Pour over balls in skillet. Stir constantly, basting balls. Cook until sauce thickens. Serve ham balls with sauce.
8. *For Sweet-Sour Sauce* — Blend brown sugar and 1 tablespoon all-purpose flour together.
9. Stir in water, vinegar, corn syrup, and cloves.
10. Remove cloves before serving.

*6 servings*
*30 min.*

# Panbroiled Lamb Chops

4 **lamb chops, cut about ¾ in. thick**
1 **teaspoon salt**
¼ **teaspoon pepper**

1. Heat a heavy skillet.
2. Set out lamb chops.
3. Place chops in skillet and brown meat slowly. Maintain a temperature which allows juices to evaporate rather than collect in pan. With too low heat, the meat will simmer in its own juices and become dry and less tender when cooked. If necessary, turn meat occasionally for even browning and pour off fat as it accumulates.
4. For each pound of meat, mix together 1 teaspoon salt and ¼ teaspoon pepper.
5. When chops are browned on one side, turn and sprinkle one-half of seasoning mixture over top. Brown other side and sprinkle remaining seasoning over it just before serving. Allow 10 to 12 min. for complete panbroiling time. Test for doneness by cutting a slit along the bone and noting color of meat.

*4 servings*
*15 min.*

**Panbroiled Beef Steaks:** Follow recipe for Panbroiled Lamb Chops. Substitute **porterhouse, sirloin, rib** or **tenderloin steaks,** 1 in. thick, for lamb chops. Allow 10 to 20 min., depending on degree of doneness desired.

*23 min.*

**Panbroiled Ham Slices:** Follow recipe for Panbroiled Lamb Chops. Substitute 1 **ham slice,** ½ in. thick for lamb chops. Omit seasoning mixture. Allow 8 to 10 min. cooking time.

*10 min.*

# Lamb Kabobs

| | |
|---|---|
| 1½ | lbs. boned lamb shoulder or leg |
| ¾ | cup tarragon vinegar |
| ⅓ | cup salad oil |
| 3 | teaspoons salt |
| ½ | teaspoon pepper |
| 1 | bay leaf |
| ½ | clove garlic |
| 6 | small (about 1 lb.) onions |
| 12 | large mushrooms |
| 6 | chicken livers |
| 3 | slices bacon |
| | Melted butter or margarine |
| ⅛ | teaspoon pepper |

1. Set out lamb shoulder or leg.
2. Cut into 1½-in. cubes. Cover lamb with marinade and set in refrigerator for at least 24 hrs., turning meat several times.
3. *For Marinade*—Mix vinegar, salad oil, 2 teaspoons salt, ½ teaspoon pepper, bay leaf, and garlic thoroughly.
4. *For Kabobs*—Set out six 8-in. skewers.
5. Clean onions, cut into halves from top to base and set aside.
6. Clean mushrooms (do not slice), remove stems and set aside. (Mushroom stems may be used in other recipes as desired.)
7. Set out chicken livers.
8. Cut bacon into halves and wrap around chicken livers.
9. Thread onto each skewer in the following order: lamb, onion half, mushroom and liver; repeat, ending with mushroom. Do not crowd pieces on skewer.
10. Brush meat and vegetables generously with butter or margarine.
11. Arrange skewers on broiler rack.
12. Set temperature control of range at broil.
13. Place broiler rack in broiler with tops of kabobs about 3 in. from source of heat. Broil 15 to 20 min., turning kabobs several times and brushing with melted butter or margarine. Test for doneness by cutting a slit in lamb cubes and noting color of meat.
14. Sprinkle kabobs with a mixture of 1 teaspoon salt and 1/8 teaspoon pepper.
15. Serve at once.

*6 servings*
*25 min.*

**Liver Kabobs:** Follow recipe for Lamb Kabobs. Substitute **veal** or **calf's liver** for lamb; cut into ¾-in. cubes. Omit marinade and chicken livers. Thread bacon, liver, onions and mushrooms alternately on skewers as desired. Broil about 10 min., or until liver is browned.

*25 min.*

**Beef Kabobs:** Follow recipe for Lamb Kabobs. Substitute tender **beef** for lamb. Omit chicken livers. Thread beef, bacon and vegetables alternately on skewers.

*25 min.*

**Scallop Kabobs:** Follow recipe for Lamb Kabobs. Substitute **scallops** for lamb. Omit marinade, chicken livers and onions. Rinse, remove and discard stem end and cut into fourths 3 small **tomatoes.** Thread the scallops, tomatoes, bacon and mushrooms alternately on skewers. Broil 5 to 10 min., or until scallops are lightly browned.

*20 min.*

**Out-of-Cupboard Kabobs:** Follow recipe for Lamb Kabobs. Substitute for lamb and chicken livers, contents of one 12 oz. can **luncheon meat,** cut in cubes. Omit marinade and bacon. Alternate meat cubes and vegetables on skewers.

*20 min.*

**Kidneys en Brochette:** Follow recipe for Lamb Kabobs. Using only **lamb kidneys** and omitting lamb, vegetables, chicken livers and bacon. Split and remove membrane (unless this has been done at market). Using scissors, remove tubes. Rinse kidneys with cold water. Marinate at least 24 hrs. Insert skewer through lamb kidneys. Broil about 10 to 15 min., or until kidneys are tender. Serve with **Tomato Sauce** (page 59).

*15 min.*

# Toasted Frankfurter Rolls

¼  **cup butter or margarine**
1  **tablespoon prepared mustard**
1  **teaspoon prepared horse-radish**
8  **slices bread**
8  **frankfurters**
   **Melted butter or margarine**
8  **tiny sweet gherkins**

1. Cream together butter or margarine, mustard, and horse-radish thoroughly and set aside.
2. Trim crust from bread.
3. Spread bread slices with creamed mixture. Place frankfurters diagonally on bread slices.
4. Pin free corners of bread together around frankfurters with wooden picks. Arrange on broiler rack. Brush tops with butter or margarine.
5. Set temperature control of range at Broil.
6. Place broiler rack in broiler with tops of rolls 4 to 5 in. from source of heat; broil until browned. Or, bake at 400°F about 20 min.
7. Fasten gherkins on the ends of the wooden picks.
8. Serve immediately.

*8 frankfurter rolls*
*20 min.*

**Frankfurter Biscuits:** Follow recipe for Toasted Frankfurter Rolls. Omit bread slices. Prepare **rolled biscuit dough** (Rolled Biscuits, page 72). Roll ¼ in. thick and spread with creamed mixture. Cut dough into wedge-shape pieces. Wrap wedges around frankfurters, starting with wide end. Place on baking sheet with points of wedges underneath. Brush dough with **milk.** Bake at 425°F about 12 min., or until biscuit rolls are golden brown.

*30 min.*

# Frilly Frankfurters

1  **cup Whipped Potatoes (one-half recipe, page 49)**
¼  **cup finely chopped onion**
¼  **cup chopped sweet pickle**
3  **tablespoons chopped pi-miento**
6  **frankfurters**
¼  **cup prepared mustard**

1. Set out an 11¾x7½x1¾-in. baking dish.
2. Prepare Whipped Potatoes.
3. Mix thoroughly with onion, pickle, and pimiento.
4. Set aside.
5. Make a lengthwise slit almost through frankfurters.
6. Open slit frankfurters and spread cut surfaces with mustard.
7. Arrange frankfurters in baking dish; pile potato mixture lightly over top.
8. Bake at 350°F 20 min.
9. Or, for broiling, arrange frankfurters on broiler rack. Pile whipped potato mixture on frankfurters.
10. Set temperature control of range at Broil.
11. Place broiler rack in broiler with top of potatoes 4 to 5 in. from source of heat; broil 7 to 8 min., or until lightly browned.

*6 servings*
*30 min.*

**Franks with Cheese Frills:** Follow recipe for Frilly Frankfurters. Omit chopped ingredients. Blend the Whipped Potatoes with ¾ cup (3 oz.) grated **Cheddar cheese.** Bake or broil.

*30 min.*

# Calf's Liver with Bacon

8    slices (about ⅓ lb.) bacon
4    slices (about 1 lb.) veal or calf's liver, cut about ½ in. thick
⅓    cup all-purpose flour
¾    teaspoon salt
¼    teaspoon pepper
3    tablespoons reserved bacon drippings

1. *For Panbroiled Bacon*—Place bacon in a large, cold skillet.
2. Cook at one time only as many slices as will lie flat in skillet. Cook slowly, turning frequently. Pour off fat as it collects; reserve fat.
3. When slices are evenly crisped and browned, remove from skillet. Drain on absorbent paper. Set aside to keep hot.
4. *For Panbroiled Liver*—Cut away tubes and outer membrane, if necessary, from veal or calf's liver.
5. Coat slices evenly with a mixture of flour, salt and pepper.
6. Return to skillet and heat drippings.
7. Place liver slices in skillet and brown both sides. Do not overcook slices. Place on warm serving plate along with bacon slices.

*4 servings*
*20 min.*

# Link Sausage and Apple Rings

16   sausage links (about 1 lb.)
2    tablespoons cold water
4    medium-size (about 1⅓ lbs.) apples
3    tablespoons reserved sausage dripppings
⅓    cup firmly packed brown sugar
½    teaspoon nutmeg

1. Place sausage links in a large, cold skillet.
2. Add cold water.
3. If skillet will not hold entire amount of sausage, cook one-half at a time. Cover and cook slowly 8 to 10 min. Remove cover and pour off liquid. Brown links over medium heat, turning as necessary (do not prick links with a fork). Pour off fat as it collects; reserve fat.
4. Meanwhile, wash and core apples.
5. Cut each apple crosswise into about 5 slices (½ to ¾ in. thick).
6. When sausage links are browned, remove from skillet. Drain on absorbent paper. Set aside to keep warm while cooking apple slices.
7. Place apple slices flat in hot skillet containing sausage drippings.
8. Cook over low heat 5 to 8 min., or until apple rings are almost tender when pierced with a fork; turn carefully.
9. Sprinkle apple rings with a mixture of brown sugar and nutmeg.
10. Cook gently until sugar is completely melted.
11. Serve with sausage links.

*4 to 6 servings*
*30 min.*

**Brussels Sprouts and Grapes 51**

# Hash on a Bun

| | |
|---|---|
| 1 | **15-oz. can corned beef hash** |
| ¼ | **cup pickle relish, drained** |
| ¼ | **cup chopped onion** |
| 2 | **teaspoons prepared horse-radish** |
| ½ | **teaspoon salt** |
| ⅛ | **teaspoon pepper** |
| 2 | **tablespoons butter or margarine** |
| | **Cheese Sauce (page 59)** |

1. Set out an 8-in. skillet.
2. Remove both ends from can and push out contents of corned beef hash.
3. Mix lightly, but thoroughly, with a mixture of pickle relish, onion, horse-radish, salt, and pepper.
4. Shape into 4 patties.
5. Heat butter or margarine in the skillet.
6. Add patties and brown slowly on both sides.
7. Meanwhile, prepare Cheese Sauce.
8. Serve patties on halves of buttered, toasted buns. Top with sauce and remaining toasted bun halves.

*4 servings*
*30 min.*

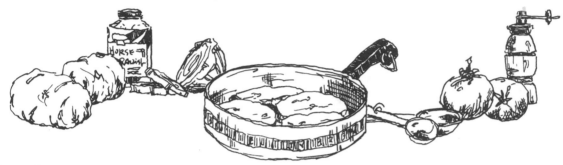

# Hash Distinctive

| | |
|---|---|
| 1 | **15-oz. can corned beef hash** |
| 2 | **teaspoons melted butter or margarine** |
| 2 | **oz. Cheddar cheese (about ½ cup, grated)** |
| 2 | **teaspoons prepared horse-radish** |
| 1 | **medium-size tomato** |
| | **Melted butter or margarine** |
| ½ | **teaspoon salt** |
| | **Few grains pepper** |

1. Remove both ends from can and push out contents of corned beef hash.
2. Cut hash evenly into 4 rounds. Place on broiler rack and brush tops with melted butter or margarine.
3. Set temperature control of range at Broil.
4. Place broiler rack in broiler with top of meat 3 in. from source of heat; broil 3 to 5 min., or until browned.
5. Grate Cheddar cheese and set aside.
6. Turn hash rounds and spread tops thinly with horse-radish.
7. Rinse tomato, remove and discard stem end and cut into four slices.
8. Place one slice on each hash round. Brush tomato slices with melted butter or margarine.
9. Sprinkle grated cheese over tomato slices. Sprinkle with a mixture of salt and pepper.
10. Broil about 5 min. longer.

*4 servings*
*20 min.*

**Hash Delectable with Pineapple Topping:** Follow recipe for Hash Distinctive. Omit horse-radish-tomato topping. Turn hash rounds and top each round with a canned **pineapple slice.** Spread with a mixture of ⅔ cup firmly packed **brown sugar** and ¼ cup softened **butter** or **margarine.** Broil about 5 min., or until pineapple is glazed. Serve immediately; garnish with **parsley.**

*20 min.*

Vegetables Polonaise 51

# Ham-Macaroni Roll-Ups

1½  qts. water
1½  teaspoons salt
4  oz. uncooked tube macaroni
2  cups Cheese Sauce (double recipe, page 59; use 14½-oz. can evaporated milk and ⅓ cup water for milk; add 1 teaspoon dry mustard with dry ingredients)
6  thin slices cooked ham

1. Grease bottom of 11¾x7½x1¾-in. baking dish.
2. Heat water and salt to boiling in a large saucepan.
3. Break tube macaroni into halves and add gradually.
4. Boil rapidly, uncovered, 10 to 15 min.
5. Test tenderness by pressing a piece against side of pan with fork or spoon. Drain macaroni by turning it into a colander or large sieve; rinse with hot water to remove loose starch.
6. While macaroni is cooking, prepare Cheese Sauce.
7. Divide macaroni into 6 bundles. Wrap ham around bundles and secure with wooden picks.
8. Arrange bundles in baking dish; pour hot Cheese Sauce over ham.
9. Set temperature control of range at Broil.
10. Place baking dish in broiler with top of ham about 4 in. from source of heat; broil about 3 min., or until lightly browned. Remove wooden picks from roll-ups before serving.

*6 servings*
*30 min.*

# Chili Con Carne

1  tablespoon fat
1  lb. ground beef
2  cups (16-oz. can, drained) kidney beans
1¼  cups (10½- to 11-oz. can) condensed tomato soup
⅓  cup hot water
1  tablespoon chili powder
1  teaspoon salt
⅛  teaspoon pepper
1  cup (about 2 medium-size) chopped onion
¼  cup chopped green pepper

1. Heat fat in a large skillet.
2. Add ground beef and cook over medium heat until browned, breaking into small pieces with a fork or spoon.
3. Meanwhile, heat kidney beans, condensed tomato soup and water in a saucepan, over medium heat, stirring occasionally.
4. Blend in a mixture of chili powder, salt and pepper.
5. Stir onion and green pepper into sauce.
6. Continue cooking sauce over medium heat while meat browns. Combine sauce with meat in skillet. Bring to boiling and simmer 10 min., stirring frequently.

*5 to 6 servings*
*30 min.*

**Chili-Spaghetti Mix:** Follow recipe for Chili con Carne. Heat 2 cups cooked **spaghetti** with chili in last 10 min. cooking period. Gently keep mixture moving with a spoon.

# Cranberry Glazed Canadian-Style Bacon

| | |
|---|---|
| 10 | slices (about 1 lb.) Canadian-style bacon, cut about ¼ in. thick |
| 1 | tablespoon grated orange peel |
| ½ | teaspoon sugar |
| ⅛ | teaspoon cloves |
| | Dash of nutmeg |
| 1 | cup whole cranberry sauce |

1. Arrange bacon in a 11¾x7½x1¾-in. baking dish.
2. Sprinkle slices with a mixture of orange peel, sugar, cloves and nutmeg.
3. Spread cranberry sauce over bacon slices.
4. Bake uncovered at 350°F about 25 min.
5. Serve with sauce spooned over bacon slices.

*5 servings*
*30 min.*

**Broiled Canadian Style Bacon:** Follow recipe for Cranberry Glazed Canadian-Style Bacon for amount of Canadian-style bacon.

Set temperature control of range at Broil. Arrange bacon slices on broiler rack. Place in broiler with top of meat 3 in. from source of heat. Broil about 10 min., or until browned. turning slices once.

Spoon about ½ cup whole **cranberry sauce** into cavities of 5 canned **peach halves** and place on broiler rack when bacon is turned. Arrange bacon around peaches on platter.

*Note:* Any **jelly** may be used to glaze Canadian-style bacon or to fill cavities of peaches.

*15 min.*

# Broiled Fish Steaks

| | |
|---|---|
| 2 | lbs. fish steaks such as cod, halibut or salmon |
| ¼ | cup butter or margarine, melted |
| 1 | tablespoon chopped parsley or chives |
| 1 | teaspoon salt |
| ⅛ | teaspoon pepper Hollandaise Sauce (page 60) |

1. Set temperature control of range at Broil and grease a broiler rack.
2. Have fish steaks ready (If using frozen steaks, thaw according to directions on pkg.) If possible, bring horse shoe ends of each steak together and fasten with a small skewer to give oval shape. Arrange steaks on the greased broiler rack. Brush tops of steaks with one-half of a mixture of butter or margarine, parsley or chives.
3. Place broiler rack in broiler with top of steaks 2 in. from source of heat; broil 5 to 8 min. (depending upon thickness of steaks). Season steaks with one-half of a mixture of salt and pepper.
4. Turn steaks carefully and brush second side with remaining butter mixture. Broil 5 to 8 min. longer, or until fish flakes easily. Sprinkle second side with remaining seasoning mixture. Remove carefully to warm serving platter.
5. Serve with lemon wedges or Hollandaise Sauce.

*6 servings*
*20 min.*

**Broiled Fish Fillets:** Follow recipe for Broiled Fish Steaks. Substitute **fish fillets** for steaks. Place skin-side down on greased rack. Broil 10 to 12 min. without turning. Brush fillets with **butter** or **margarine** during broiling.

*Note:* Steaks are cross-section slices of fish. Fish fillets are flat slices cut lengthwise from sides of fish.

*20 min.*

# Creamy Curried Shrimp

| | |
|---|---|
| 3 | cups **Perfection Boiled Rice** (page 60) |
| 1 | **4-oz. can sliced mushrooms** (about ½ cup, drained) |
| 2 | **5-oz. cans shrimp** (about 1½ cups, drained) **Milk** |
| 1½ | cups (about ¾ lb.) **diced, cooked ham** |
| ¼ | cup **butter or margarine** |
| ¼ | cup **finely chopped onion** |
| ¼ | cup **finely chopped celery** |
| ¼ | cup **all-purpose flour** |
| 1 | teaspoon **curry powder** |
| ½ | teaspoon **salt** |
| ⅛ | teaspoon **pepper** |

1. Set out a 2-qt. saucepan.
2. Prepare 3 cups Perfection Boiled Rice and keep hot.
3. Meanwhile, drain, reserving liquid, contents of mushrooms and shrimp.
4. Remove black veins from shrimp. Set mushrooms and shrimp aside.
5. Add milk to mushroom and shrimp liquids enough to make 2 cups liquid.
6. Set aside.
7. Dice enough cooked ham to yield 1½ cups.
8. Set aside.
9. Melt butter or margarine in the saucepan over low heat.
10. Add and cook onion and celery over medium heat about 5 min., stirring occasionally.
11. Blend in a mixture of flour, curry powder, salt and pepper.
12. Heat until mixture bubbles, stirring constantly. Remove from heat. Add gradually and stir liquid into mixture. Return to heat and bring mixture rapidly to boiling, stirring constantly. Cook until sauce thickens.
13. Blend mushrooms, shrimp and ham into sauce.
14. Cook a few min. longer until shrimp and ham are heated keeping mixture moving gently with a spoon.
15. Serve over hot rice on a warm serving platter.

*4 servings*
*30 min.*

# Cooked Shrimp

| | |
|---|---|
| 1 | lb. **fresh shrimp with shells** |
| 1 | pt. **water** |
| 3 | tablespoons **lemon juice** |
| 1 | tablespoon **salt** **Peppy Cocktail Sauce** (page 14) |

1. Wash shrimp in cold water.
2. Drop shrimp into a boiling mixture of water, lemon juice and salt.
3. Cover tightly. Simmer 5 min., or only until shrimp are pink and tender. Drain and cover with cold water to chill. Drain shrimp again.
4. Remove tiny legs. Peel shells from shrimp. Cut a slit to just below surface along back (curved surface) of shrimp to expose the back vein. With knife point remove vein in one piece. Rinse quickly in cold running water.
5. Serve cooked shrimp in creamed mixtures, shrimp salad, or as an appetizer with Peppy Cocktail Sauce.

*½ lb. Cooked Shrimp*
*25 min.*

*Note:* Veins present in canned or frozen shrimp are removed in the same way.

*25 min.*

# Tuna-Stuffed Peppers

4   large green peppers
1   cup Medium White Sauce
    (page 58; use cream for
    milk)
1   teaspoon lemon juice
½   teaspoon paprika
1   7-oz. can tuna fish or
    7¾-oz. can salmon
¼   cup (1-oz.) grated
    Parmesan or Cheddar
    cheese

1. Grease a 2-qt. baking dish.
2. Rinse and slice stem ends from peppers.
3. With a knife or spoon, remove and discard white fiber and seeds. Rinse cavities. Drop into boiling salted water to cover and simmer 5 min. Remove peppers from water and invert. Set aside to drain.
4. Meanwhile, prepare medium white sauce.
5. Blend lemon juice and paprika into sauce and set aside.
6. Drain and flake tuna fish or salmon with a fork.
7. Combine with sauce; spoon mixture into peppers. Place in baking dish.
8. Bake at 350°F about 15 min. Just before serving, sprinkle with Parmesan or Cheddar cheese.
9. Other kinds of fish may be used, or combinations of several kinds.

*4 servings*
*30 min.*

**Rice-Stuffed Pepper:** Follow recipe for Tuna-Stuffed Peppers. Substitute **Tomato Sauce** for Medium White Sauce. Substitute ½ lb. **ground beef** for tuna fish. Brown ground beef in 2 tablespoons **shortening,** breaking it into small pieces with fork or spoon.
Prepare ⅔ cup package **precooked rice** according to directions on package. Mix with sauce and browned meat. Heap mixture into peppers and bake as in Tuna-Stuffed Peppers.

*30 min.*

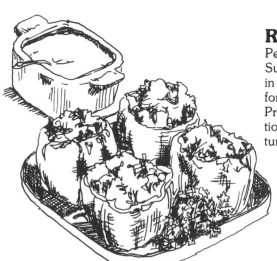

# Panfried Fish Fillets

2   lbs. fish fillets
1   cup (3 slices) fine, dry
    bread crumbs
1   tablespoon grated
    Parmesan cheese
2   teaspoons salt
⅛   teaspoon pepper
2   eggs
2   tablespoons milk
    Olive oil
½   clove garlic, crushed (in a
    garlic press or in mortar
    with pestle)
    Maitre d'Hotel Butter
    (page 60)

1. Set out a large skillet.
2. Set out fish fillets (If using frozen fish fillets, allow additional time for thawing. Thaw according to directions on package.) Cut into serving-size pieces and set fillets aside.
3. Mix bread crumbs, Parmesan cheese, salt and pepper in a shallow pan and set aside.
4. Beat eggs lightly in a shallow dish.
5. Heat enough olive oil in the skillet to make a layer ¼ in. deep.
6. Add garlic.
7. Dip fillets into egg mixture, then coat with crumb mixture. When oil is hot, panfry fish over moderate heat. Cook one side until crisp and browned. Turn carefully with spatula or pancake turner and brown other side. Allow 8 to 12 min. total cooking time, depending upon thickness of fillets.
8. Serve with Maitre d'Hotel Butter.

*6 servings*
*20 min.*

# Leftover Special

Rolled Biscuits (page 72; blend ¼ teaspoon marjoram into dry ingredients)
2   cups diced turkey
1¾  cups leftover gravy
2   tablespoons chopped onion
1   egg yolk, slightly beaten
    Salt and pepper to taste (depending upon amount of seasoning in gravy)

1. Set out a baking sheet and a 1-qt. saucepan.
2. Prepare dough for rolled biscuits.
3. Roll biscuit dough into a rectangle ¼ in. thick. Set aside while preparing filling.
4. *For Filling*—Have ready turkey, gravy and onion and set aside.
5. Heat in saucepan ¾ cup of the leftover gravy. Vigorously stir about 3 tablespoons hot gravy into egg yolk.
6. Immediately blend into hot gravy and cook 2 to 3 min. Blend in 1 cup of the diced turkey, chopped onion, salt and pepper.
7. Spread filling on biscuit dough. Starting with long side of dough, roll; pinch ends to seal. Place on baking sheet.
8. Bake at 450°F 10 to 15 min.
9. Meanwhile, heat together in a saucepan remaining turkey and gravy. Serve over roll.

*6 servings*
*30 min.*

**Leftover De Luxe:** Follow recipe for Leftover Special. While turkey roll is baking, prepare **Fried Mushrooms** (page 46). Stir into turkey-gravy mixture to be served over roll.

*30 min.*

# Dried Beef in Toast Cups

4   Hard-Cooked Eggs
6   Toast Cups (page 18)
2   cups Medium White Sauce (double recipe, page 58)
4   oz. can sliced mushrooms (about ½ cup, drained)
1   cup (about 2½ oz.) dried beef, shredded
¼   cup chopped parsley

1. Prepare eggs and toast cups.
2. Meanwhile, prepare medium white sauce and keep hot.
3. Force egg yolks through a sieve or ricer and set aside for a garnish.
4. Chop egg whites and set aside.
5. Drain contents of can sliced mushrooms.
6. Stir mushrooms and chopped egg whites into sauce with dried beef and parsley.
7. Cook mixture a few min. to heat thoroughly, stirring occasionally. Spoon into Toast Cups. Sprinkle sieved egg yolks over tops.
8. Serve immediately.

*6 servings*
*30 min.*

# Welsh Rabbit

4   cups (1 lb.) grated sharp Cheddar cheese
½   cup milk
½   teaspoon dry mustard
½   teaspoon Worcestershire sauce
    Dash of cayenne pepper
    Buttered toast points or melba toast

1. Heat cheese and milk in top of double boiler over simmering water until cheese is melted, stirring constantly.
2. Stir in dry mustard, Worcestershire sauce and cayenne pepper.
3. Pour cheese mixture over buttered toast points or melba toast.
4. Top each serving with a tomato slice and serve immediately.

*6 servings*
*20 min.*

**Tomato-Cheese Rabbit:** Follow recipe for Welsh Rabbit. Decrease cheese to 2 cups (½ lb.). Substitute 1¼ cups (10½ to 11-oz. can) **condensed tomato soup** for milk. Vigorously stir about 3 tablespoons hot mixture into 1 **egg,** slightly beaten. Return to double boiler and add seasonings. Cook 3 to 5 min. longer, stirring constantly.

*20 min.*

# Double-Quick Baked Beans

| | |
|---|---|
| 1 | tablespoon butter or margarine |
| ¼ | cup chopped onion |
| ¼ | cup ketchup |
| 2 | tablespoons molasses |
| 2 | drops Tabasco |
| 2 | tablespoons brown sugar |
| ½ | teaspoon salt |
| ½ | teaspoon dry mustard |
| 2 | cups (1 16-oz. can) baked beans |
| 4 | slices bacon |

1. Heat four individual casseroles in oven.
2. Melt butter or margarine in a skillet.
3. Add onion and cook over medium heat until soft, stirring occasionally.
4. Blend in ketchup, molasses, Tabasco, brown sugar, salt and dry mustard.
5. Bring to boiling. Stir in baked beans.
6. Turn mixture into casseroles.
7. Cut bacon crosswise into pieces.
8. Put several pieces on top of bean mixture in each casserole.
9. Bake at 375°F about 20 min., or until bacon is cooked.
10. Serve with **Boston brown bread.**

*4 servings*
*30 min.*

# Jiffy Creamed Chicken

| | |
|---|---|
| 3 | slices bread |
| 3 | tablespoons melted butter or margarine |
| 1 | 16-oz. can peas (about 1½ cups, drained) |
| | Boned chicken (13-oz. can), cut in pieces |
| 1¼ | cups (10½-to11- oz. can) condensed cream of mushroom soup |
| ⅓ | cup reserved liquid |
| ½ | teaspoon salt |
| ⅛ | teaspoon pepper |

1. Grease and set aside a 1½-qt. casserole or a 10-in. pie pan.
2. Cut bread with a small chicken-shape cookie cutter, or cut into cubes.
3. Toss bread cubes in, or brush cut-outs with melted butter or margarine.
4. Set aside.
5. Drain peas reserving liquid, and place in a large saucepan.
6. Blend in and heat thoroughly chicken, cream of mushroom soup, reserved liquid, salt and pepper.
7. Turn into the casserole or pie pan. Top with buttered bread.
8. Bake at 400°F 15 min., or until bread is browned.

*6 servings*
*30 min.*

*Note:* If mixture seems too thick, gradually add some of the remaining reserved liquid.

# Perfection Boiled Rice

2   qts. water
1   tablespoon salt
1   cup rice

1. Bring water and salt to boiling in a deep saucepan.
2. So boiling will not stop, add rice gradually to water.
3. (The Rice Industry no longer considers it necessary to wash rice before cooking.) Boil rapidly, uncovered, 15 to 20 min., or until a kernel is entirely soft when pressed between fingers.
4. Drain rice in colander or sieve and rinse with hot water to remove loose starch. Cover colander and rice with a clean towel and set over hot water until rice kernels are dry and fluffly.

*About 3 cups cooked rice*
*30 min.*

## Quick Cooking Rice

Cooked rice prepared from packaged **precooked rice** may be substituted for Perfection Boiled Rice if directions on the package are followed carefully for amounts and timing.

# Quick Rice Ring

3   cups Perfection Boiled Rice
    Finely chopped parsley
    Jiffy Creamed Chicken (page 39, omit bread, butter, and baking)
    Dried Beef in Toast Cups (page 18)

1. Lightly butter a 1-qt. ring mold.
2. Prepare rice.
3. Turn cooked rice into prepared mold, pack down gently with a spoon. Invert onto a warm serving platter and lift off mold. Sprinkle rice ring with parsley.
4. Fill rice ring with a buttered cooked vegetable or any creamed mixture of meat, fish or poultry.
5. For Jiffy Creamed Chicken Ring—While rice is cooking, prepare Jiffy Cream Chicken.
6. Fill rice ring with creamed chicken mixture.
7. For Dried Beef in Rice Ring—While rice is cooking, prepare (omit Toast Cups) Dried Beef in Toast Cups.
8. Fill rice ring with dried beef mixture.

*4 to 6 servings*
*30 min.*

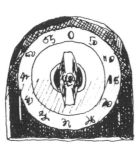

# EGGS

## *Cheese Puffy Omelets*

| | |
|---|---|
| **4** | **oz. process American cheese (1 cup, grated)** |
| **3** | **egg yolks** |
| **3** | **egg whites** |
| **3** | **tablespoons water** |
| **½** | **teaspoon salt** |
| | **Few grains white pepper** |
| **2** | **tablespoons butter or margarine** |
| | **Paprika** |

1. Set oven temperature control of range at 350°F.
2. Set out a griddle or a heavy 10-in. skillet.
3. Grate cheese and set aside.
4. Beat egg yolks until thick and lemon colored.
5. Set aside.
6. Using clean beaters, beat egg whites until frothy.
7. Add water, salt and pepper to egg whites.
8. Continue beating egg white mixture until rounded peaks are formed.
9. Melt butter or margarine on griddle or in skillet until bubbling hot.
10. Spread egg yolks over egg whites and fold gently together. Slide gently into three equal portions onto hot griddle or as one large omelet into skillet. Cook ½ min.; lower heat and cook slowly about 10 min., or until lightly browned on bottom. Do not stir at any time. Mixture will look moist and puffy on top.
11. Place griddle with omelets or skillet with omelet into 350°F oven about 5 min. Sprinkle one-third of the grated cheese over the top of each small omelet or all of the cheese over the large omelet.
12. Return omelets to oven and continue baking until cheese melts. To serve, loosen edges with spatula, make a quick, shallow cut through center and fold one side over. Gently slip onto a warm serving platter. Garnish with paprika.
13. Serve immediately.

*3 servings*
*30 min.*

**Fruit Juice Omelet:** Follow recipe for Cheese Puffy Omelets. Omit cheese. Substitute **orange juice** for water. Or, decrease water to 2 tablespoons and add with 2 teaspoons **lemon juice** to egg whites.

*25 min.*

**Cottage Cheese Omelet:** Follow recipe for Cheese Puffy Omelets. Omit cheese. Combine with egg mixture ½ cup **cottage cheese,** 1 tablespoon finely chopped **pimiento** and 2 teaspoons minced **chives.**

*25 min.*

# Soft-Cooked Eggs

4    **eggs**

1. Put eggs into a saucepan and cover with cold or lukewarm water.
2. Cover. Bring water rapidly to boiling. Turn off heat. If necessary to prevent further boiling, remove saucepan from source of heat. Let stand covered 2 to 4 min., depending upon firmness desired.

*4 Soft-Cooked Eggs*
*5 min.*

*Note:* Eggs are a protein food and therefore should never be boiled.

**Hard-Cooked Eggs:** Follow recipe for Soft-Cooked Eggs. After bringing water to boiling, let eggs stand covered 20 to 22 min. Plunge cooked eggs promptly into running cold water. Immediately crackle shells under water. Roll egg between hands to loosen shell. When cooled, start peeling at large end.

*25 min.*

# Poached Eggs

¼    **teaspoon salt**
4    **eggs**

1. Grease bottom of a heavy, shallow pan or skillet. Pour in hot water to 2-in. depth or enough to rise 1 in. above tops of eggs.
2. Add salt to water.
3. Bring water to boiling and then reduce heat to keep water simmering.
4. Break eggs separately into a saucer or small dish.
5. Tilting dish toward edge of pan, quickly slip each egg into water; do not crowd. Cook 3 to 5 min., depending upon firmness desired. Carefully remove eggs with slotted pancake turner or spoon. To drain, hold spoon on folded paper napkin a few seconds.
6. Serve immediately on hot buttered toast or with vegetables. Season with salt, pepper and butter or margarine.

*4 Poached Eggs*
*10 min.*

**Eggs Benedict:** Follow recipe for Poached Eggs. Cover toasted, buttered **English muffin halves** with thin, round slices of hot **ham.** Place a poached egg on each ham round and top with **Hollandaise Sauce** (page 60; allow about ¼ cup sauce per serving).

*30 min.*

# Scrambled Eggs

**6** eggs
**6** tablespoons milk, cream or undiluted evaporated milk
**¾** teaspoon salt
**⅛** teaspoon pepper
**3** tablespoons butter or margarine

1. Set out an 8 to 10-in. skillet.
2. Put into a bowl eggs, milk, salt and pepper.
3. For uniform yellow color, beat egg mixture until thoroughly blended. For streaks, beat only slightly.
4. Heat skillet until just hot enough to sizzle a drop of water. Melt butter or margarine.
5. Pour in egg mixture and cook slowly over low heat. With a fork or spatula, lift mixture from bottom and sides of skillet as it thickens, allowing uncooked part to flow to bottom. Avoid stirring. Cook slowly until scrambled eggs are thick and creamy throughout but are still moist.
6. If desired, add minced parsley or chives to egg mixture. Serve immediately.

*4 servings*
*15 min.*

**Egg and Cheese Scramble:** Follow recipe for Scrambled Eggs. Allow eggs to thicken slightly at first. Then mix in ¼ cup (1 oz.) grated Cheddar cheese.

*20 min.*

**Scramble Eggs De Luxe:** Follow recipe for Scrambled Eggs. Beat with the eggs ½ teaspoon **Worcestershire sauce.** Scramble with egg mixture, ¼ cup (1 oz.) grated **cheese** and 1 medium-size **tomato,** rinsed, stem ends removed, peeled and cubed. Cook until thick and creamy. Stir in 1 cup **Croutons** (page 18).

*30 min.*

**Scrambled Eggs and Mushrooms:** Follow recipe for Scrambled Eggs. Clean and slice 6 fresh, medium-size **mushrooms.** Cook slowly about 5 min. in ¼ cup **butter** or **margarine.** Add egg mixture to mushrooms and butter in skillet.

*20 min.*

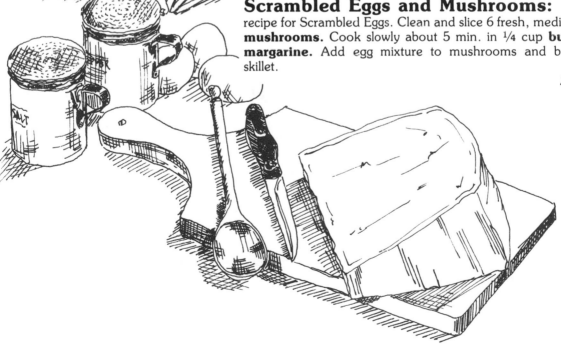

# French Omelet

6   **eggs**
6   **tablespoons milk or water**
¾   **teaspoon salt**
⅛   **teaspoon pepper**
3   **tablespoons butter or margarine**

1. Set out an 8-to 10-in. skillet.
2. Beat together eggs, milk or water, salt and pepper until well blended but not foamy.
3. Heat skillet until just hot enough to sizzle a drop of water. Melt butter or margarine in skillet.
4. Pour egg mixture into skillet and reduce heat. As edges of omelet begin to thicken, with a spoon or fork draw cooked portions toward center to allow uncooked mixture to flow to bottom of skillet. Shake and tilt skillet as necessary to aid flow of uncooked eggs. Do not stir.
5. When eggs no longer flow but surface is still moist, the heat should be increased to brown quickly the bottom of omelet. Loosen edges carefully and fold in half. Slide omelet onto a warm serving platter.
6. If desired, fill omelet before folding with diced or shredded cooked meat or vegetables.

*4 to 6 servings*
*20 min.*

**Mushroom Omelet:** Drain, reserving liquid, contents of 8-oz. can **mushroom pieces and stems** (about 1 cup, drained). Cook mushrooms until lightly browned in a small skillet containing 3 tablespoons **butter** or **margarine.** Set aside and keep warm. Follow recipe for French Omelet, substituting **mushroom liquid** for milk or water. Spoon mushrooms over top of omelet just before folding.

*20 min.*

**Cheese Omelet:** Follow recipe for French Omelet. Blend ¼ cup (1 oz.) grated **Swiss** or **Cheddar cheese** and 2 tablespoons minced **parsley** into egg mixture before pouring into skillet. Sprinkle an additional ¼ cup (1 oz.) grated **cheese** over omelet while it is cooking.

*25 min.*

**Jam or Jelly Omelet:** Follow recipe for French Omelet. Just before folding omelet in half, spread omelet with ⅓ to ½ cup **apricot, strawberry** or **rasberry jam, orange marmalade, currant** or **cranberry jelly.**

*20 min.*

# Crepes Benedict

12   **eggs**
    **Salt and pepper**
2   **tablespoons butter or margarine**
8   **thin slices boiled ham, heated**
8   **dinner crepes**
1   **cup hollandaise (page 60)**

1. Beat eggs with salt and pepper to taste.
2. Melt butter. Soft-scramble eggs in butter.
3. To assemble, put 1 slice of ham on each crepe and spoon eggs on top. Fold crepe and ham over eggs and serve topped with warm hollandaise.

*8 filled crepes*
*15 min.*

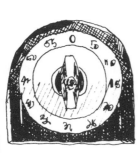

# VEGETABLES

## Tart Green Beans with Bacon

| | |
|---|---|
| 1 | lb. green beans |
| 4 | slices bacon, cut in ½-in. pieces |
| ⅓ | cup finely chopped onion |
| 2 | tablespoons vinegar |
| 2 | tablespoons water |
| 2 | tablespoons sugar |
| ¼ | teaspoon salt |
| | Dash of pepper |

1. Wash, cut off ends and cut green beans into crosswise pieces.
2. Cook 15 to 20 min., or until tender. (Frozen or canned green beans may be substituted for fresh beans. Follow directions on package or container for cooking.)
3. Meanwhile, panbroil 4 slices bacon, cut in ½-in. pieces (see Calf's Liver with Bacon, page 32) in a skillet.
4. Add to skillet onion, vinegar, water, sugar, salt and pepper.
5. Bring to boiling.
6. Drain cooked beans. Pour bacon mixture over beans and toss lightly together.

*4 servings*
*30 min.*

## Harvard Beets

| | |
|---|---|
| 1 | 16-oz. can diced beets (about 1½ cups, drained) |
| 2 | tablespoons sugar |
| 1 | tablespoon cornstarch |
| ½ | teaspoon salt |
| | Few grains pepper |
| ¾ | cup reserved beet liquid |
| 3 | tablespoons vinegar |
| 2 | tablespoons butter or margarine |

1. Drain reserving liquid, contents of can diced beets.
2. Mix together in a saucepan sugar, cornstarch, salt and pepper.
3. Stir in beet liquid and vinegar.
4. Bring to boiling, stirring constantly. Add beets and butter or margarine.
5. Again bring to boiling, stirring gently and constantly. Simmer 8 to 10 min.

*4 to 5 servings*
*20 min.*

**Beets in Orange Sauce:** Follow recipe for Harvard Beets. Decrease beet liquid to ½ cup. Substitute ⅓ cup **orange juice** for vinegar. Add ¼ teaspoon grated **orange peel.** Garnish with **Hard-Cooked Eggs,** chopped.

*20 min.*

# Candied Carrots

| | |
|---|---|
| 6 | medium-size (about 1½ lbs.) carrots |
| ¾ | cup firmly packed brown sugar |
| 6 | tablespoons water |
| 3 | tablespoons butter or margarine |

1. Set out a small baking dish.
2. Wash carrots and pare or scrape.
3. Cook whole carrots 15 to 25 min., or until just tender.
4. Meanwhile, combine brown sugar, water and butter or margarine in a small saucepan.
5. Stirring constantly, cook over medium heat until sugar is dissolved. Drain carrots and place in baking dish. Cover with sugar mixture.
6. Bake at 350°F about 10 min., or until carrots are completely glazed; baste occasionally.

*6 servings*
*30 min.*

**Glazed Carrots:**  Follow recipe for Candied Carrots. Prepare whole carrots or cut lengthwise into sticks. Omit brown sugar mixture. Drain cooked carrots and dry thoroughly on absorbent paper. Melt 1½ tablespoons **butter** or **margarine** in skillet. Stir in 3 tablespoons **sugar.** With skillet over low heat, turn carrots in mixture until coated.

*20 min.*

# Pineapple Glazed Carrots

| | |
|---|---|
| 1 | 16-oz. can sliced carrots (about 2 cups, drained) |
| 1 | 9-oz. can pineapple tidbits (about ⅔ cup, drained) |
| 2 | teaspoons cornstarch |
| ½ | teaspoon salt |
| ⅔ | cup reserved carrot liquid |
| ⅓ | cup reserved pineapple syrup |
| 1 | tablespoon butter or margarine |

1. Set out a 1½-qt. saucepan.
2. Drain, reserving liquids, contents of can sliced carrots, and can pineapple tidbits.
3. Combine cornstarch and salt in the saucepan.
4. Mix carrot liquid and pineapple syrup and add gradually to cornstarch mixture, stirring constantly.
5. Bring to boiling. Stirring constantly, cook about 3 min., or until the liquid is thick and clear. Stir in butter or margarine.
6. Add carrots and pineapple. Heat thoroughly.

*4 or 5 servings*
*15 min.*

# Fried Mushrooms

| | |
|---|---|
| ½ | lb. mushrooms |
| ¼ | cup butter or margarine |
| 1 | teaspoon minced parsley |

1. Clean and slice mushrooms.
2. Heat butter or margarine in a skillet.
3. Add mushrooms to skillet. Cook slowly, occasionally moving and turning gently with a spoon, until mushrooms are tender and lightly browned. Sprinkle with minced parsley.
4. Put mushrooms in a warm dish and serve immediately.

*2 servings*
*15 min.*

# Fried Eggplant

| | |
|---|---|
| 1 | medium-size (about 1 lb.) eggplant |
| 1 | egg, slightly beaten |
| 1½ | teaspoons salt |
| ¼ | teaspoon pepper |
| ¾ | cup fine cracker crumbs |
| ¼ | cup fat |

1. Set out a large, heavy skillet.
2. Wash, pare and cut eggplant into ¼-in. slices.
3. Dip slices into a mixture of egg, salt and pepper.
4. Coat with cracker crumbs.
5. Melt fat in skillet over medium heat.
6. Add as many eggplant slices at one time as will lie flat in skillet. Cook about 15 min., or until crisp and browned, turning several times. Add extra fat when necessary.

*6 servings*
*25 min.*

**Fried Eggplant and Tomatoes:** Follow recipe for Fried Eggplant. Wash 4 firm ripe or green **tomatoes;** remove stem ends. Cut into ½-in. slices. Coat with a mixture of ½ cup **all-purpose flour,** 1 teaspoon **salt,** and 1/8 teaspoon **pepper.** Remove eggplant to warm platter when browned; keep hot. Add tomatoes to skillet and brown lightly on both sides; serve on eggplant.

*30 min.*

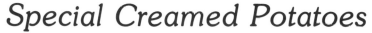

# Special Creamed Potatoes

| | |
|---|---|
| 3 | oz. sharp Cheddar cheese (about ¾ cup, grated) |
| 4 | medium-size (about 1⅓ lbs.) potatoes |
| 1 | cup water |
| 1 | teaspoon salt |
| ½ | cup (about 1 medium-size) chopped onion |
| ½ | cup milk |
| ⅛ | teaspoon pepper |

1. Grate Cheddar cheese and set aside.
2. Wash, pare and dice potatoes.
3. Bring water and salt to boiling in a saucepan.
4. Add potatoes with onion.
5. Cover and cook 10 min. Uncover and continue cooking slowly until almost all the water is evaporated. Turn occasionally and move gently with a spoon.
6. Remove from heat. Blend in grated cheese, milk and pepper.
7. Heat and stir until cheese is melted.

*6 servings*
*25 min.*

**Scalloped Potatoes:** Follow recipe for Special Creamed Potatoes. Grease 1-qt. casserole. Substitute 4 **cooked potatoes,** thinly sliced, for raw potatoes. Increase milk to ¾ cup and scald. Meanwhile, alternate in casserole layers of potatoes with layers of onion, cheese and seasoning mixture. Pour scalded milk over potatoes. Bake at 350°F about 20 min., or until potatoes are lightly browned.

*30 min.*

# Country Fried Potatoes

**6**  slices panbroiled bacon
(see Calf's Liver with
Bacon, page 32)
**6**  cold, cooked potatoes
¼  cup bacon drippings
¾  teaspoon salt
½  teapoon paprika
⅛  teaspoon pepper

1. Prepare bacon in a skillet.
2. Set aside on absorbent paper to drain.
3. Peel and slice potatoes.
4. Return bacon dripping to the skillet.
5. Add potato slices to skillet. Sprinkle with a mixture of salt, paprika and pepper
6. Cook potatoes over medium heat, turning only occasionally, until potatoes are well browned. Crumble the bacon and mix with potatoes just before serving.

*6 servings*
*20 min.*

# French Fried Potatoes

Lard
**6**  medium-size potatoes
(about 2 lbs.)
Salt

1. *Method 1*—About 20 min. before deep-frying, fill a deep saucepan one-half to two-thirds full with lard.
2. Heat slowly to 300°F.
3. Meanwhile, wash and pare potatoes.
4. Cut potatoes with knife or fancy cutter. Trim off sides and ends to form slices; stack. Cut lengthwise into sticks about ⅜in. slices; stack evenly. Cut lengthwise into sticks about ⅜in. wide. Pat dry with absorbent paper.
5. Fry about 1 cup at a time in hot fat until potatoes are tender but not browned. Remove from fat and drain on absorbent paper. Just before serving, heat fat to 360°F. Return potatoes to fat, frying 1 cup at a time. Fry until crisp and golden brown. Drain on absorbent paper. Sprinkle with salt.
6. Serve immediately or keep warm in 300°F oven.

*6 servings*
*30 min.*

1. *Method 2*—Fill a deep saucepan with fat as in Method 1 and heat to 360°F.
2. Meanwhile, wash, pare and cut potatoes as in Method 1. Fry until tender and golden brown. Drain on absorbent paper. Sprinkle with salt. Keep warm until ready to serve.

**Crepes Benedict 44**

# Gold Rush Fries

8   medium-size (about 2 to
     2½ lbs.) potatoes (6 cups,
     sliced)
⅓   cup butter or margarine
1¼  teaspoons salt
⅛   teaspoon pepper

1. Set out a heavy skillet having a cover.
2. Wash potatoes, pare and cut into extra-thin, crosswise slices.
3. Heat butter or margarine in skillet.
4. Add potato slices to skillet and sprinkle with a mixture of salt and pepper.
5. Cover and cook slowly, without turning, 10 to 15 min., or until potatoes are golden brown and crisp. Turn potatoes with spatula or turner. Continue to cook slowly, uncovered, about 15 min. longer, or until second side is browned.

*6 servings*
*30 min.*

# Whipped Potatoes

4   medium-size (about 1⅓
     lbs.) potatoes, cut in
     quarters
2   tablespoons butter or
     margarine
⅓   cup hot milk
1   teaspoon salt
⅛   teaspoon white pepper

1. Wash potatoes, pare and cook covered in boiling salted water to cover.
2. Cook about 20 min., or until potatoes are tender when pierced with a fork. Drain.
3. To dry potatoes, shake pan over low heat. To heat potato masher, food mill or ricer and a mixing bowl, scald them with boiling water.
4. Mash or rice potatoes thoroughly. Whip in butter or margarine and milk and a mixture of salt and white pepper until potatoes are fluffy.
5. Whip potatoes until light and fluffy. If necessary, keep potatoes hot over simmering water and cover with folded towel until ready to serve.

*About 2 cups Whipped Potatoes*
*30 min.*

**Vegetable Whip:** Follow recipe for Whipped Potatoes. Add hot cooked **vegetable** to mashed or riced potatoes before adding other ingredients.
For Carrot Whip—Wash, pare or scrape and cook, 4 medium-size (about 1 lb.) **carrots;** drain. Rice the cooked carrots with potatoes.
For Spinach Whip—Wash and cook ½ lb. **spinach.** Drain. Mince spinach and mix with potatoes.
For Rutabaga Whip—Use 1 cup hot cooked **rutabaga.** Rice with potatoes.

*30 min.*

**Avocados Stuffed with Cauliflower Salad 57**

# Whipped Sweet Potatoes

| | |
|---|---|
| 6 | medium-size (about 2 lbs.) sweet potatoes, cut in quarters |
| 2 | tablespoons butter or margarine |
| ½ | cup hot milk or cream |
| ½ | teaspoon salt |

1. Wash and cook potatoes covered in boiling salted water to cover.
2. Cook about 20 min., or until potatoes are tender when pierced with a fork. Drain and peel sweet potatoes.
3. To dry potatoes, shake pan over low heat. To heat potato masher, food mill or ricer and a mixing bowl, scald them with boiling water.
4. Mash or rice potatoes thoroughly. Whip in butter or margarine, milk or cream and salt until potatoes are fluffy.
5. Whip potatoes until light and fluffy. If necessary, keep potatoes hot over simmering water and cover with folded towel until ready to serve.

*About 3 cups whipped potatoes*
*30 min.*

**Mellow Sweet Potato Bake:** Follow recipe for Whipped Sweet Potatoes. Grease a 1½-qt. baking dish. Substitute **orange juice** for milk or cream. Blend into whipped potatoes a mixture of ½ cup (about 2 oz.) chopped **pecans,** ⅓ cup firmly packed **brown sugar,** 1 teaspoon **cinnamon,** and ½ teaspoon **nutmeg.** Spoon into baking dish. Cut 6 **marshmallows** into halves; arrange them on top of potatoes. Set temperature control of range at Broil. Put baking dish in broiler with top of food 4 in. from heat source. Broil until marshmallows are delicately browned and slightly melted.

*30 min.*

# Gourmet Spinach

| | |
|---|---|
| 1 | lb. spinach |
| ¼ | cup cream |
| 2 | tablespoons butter or margarine |
| 1 | tablespoon minced onion |
| 1 | teaspoon prepared horse-radish |
| ½ | teaspoon salt |
| ⅛ | teaspoon pepper |

1. Remove stems, roots, and bruised leaves from spinach.
2. Wash thoroughly by lifting up and down in cold water. Lift leaves out of water each time. When free from sand and gritty material, place spinach in heavy saucepan. Cook 8 to 10 min.
3. Drain cooked spinach and chop. Return spinach to saucepan. Add cream, butter or margarine, onion, horse-radish and a mixture of salt and pepper and stir to blend.
4. Return to heat; cook until heated thoroughly.

*4 servings*
*25 min.*

**Spinach-Cheese Ramekins:** Follow recipe for Gourmet Spinach. Set out 6 ramekins or individual baking dishes. Omit cream, onion and horse-radish. While spinach is cooking, prepare **Welsh Rabbit** (one-half recipe, page 38). Add butter or margarine and seasonings to spinach and spoon equal portions into ramekins. Pour Welsh Rabbit over tops. Sprinkle with ⅔ cup buttered, crushed **corn flakes.** Bake at 350°F about 10 min.

*30 min.*

# Vegetables Polonaise

1½   pounds vegetables (Brussels sprouts or savoy cabbage or carrots or cauliflower or green beans or leeks)
1   cup boiling water
1   teaspoon salt
½   teaspoon sugar (optional)
2   tablespoons butter
¼   teaspoon salt
⅛   teaspoon pepper
1   tablespoon lemon juice (optional)
2   tablespoons fine dry bread crumbs

1. Choose one vegetable to prepare at a time. Trim and pare as necessary. (Leave Brussels sprouts and green beans whole. Cut cabbage into six wedges. Leave cauliflower whole or break into flowerets. Slice leeks.)
2. Cook vegetable, covered, in boiling water with 1 teaspoon salt and the sugar, if desired, until tender. Drain off water.
3. Melt butter. Stir in ¼ teaspoon salt, pepper, and lemon juice. Add bread crumbs. Saute until golden. Spoon over top of vegetable.

*About 4 servings*
*30 min.*

# Noodles and Cabbage

¼   cup butter or magarine
½   cup chopped onion
4   cups chopped or sliced cabbage
1   teaspoon caraway seed
½   teaspoon salt
⅛   teaspoon pepper
1   package (8 ounces) egg noodles
½   cup dairy sour cream (optional)

1. Melt butter in a large skillet. Add onion; saute until soft.
2. Add cabbage; saute 5 minutes, or until crisp-tender. Stir in caraway seed, salt, and pepper.
3. Meanwhile, cook noodles in salted boiling water as directed on package. Drain well.
4. Stir noodles into cabbage. Add sour cream, if desired. Cook 5 minutes longer, stirring frequently.

*6 to 8 servings*
*30 min.*

# Brussels Sprouts and Grapes

1½   pounds fresh Brussels sprouts, cut in half
1½   cups beer
2   teaspoons melted butter
¼   teaspoon salt
⅛   teaspoon freshly ground white pepper
1   cup seedless white grapes
  Snipped parsley

1. Simmer Brussels sprouts in beer in covered saucepan until tender (about 8 minutes); drain.
2. Drizzle butter over sprouts; sprinkle with salt and pepper. Add grapes; heat thoroughly. Sprinkle with parsley.

*4 to 6 servings*
*15 min.*

# SALADS

## Peach Blush Salad

| | |
|---|---|
| 8 | medium-size canned peach halves (17-oz. can) |
| 1 | pkg. (3 oz.) cream cheese |
| ¼ | cup mayonnaise |
| ½ | teaspoon prepared horse-radish |
| ¼ | teaspoon salt |
| ¼ | cup (about 1½ oz.) chopped almonds |
| ¼ | cup chopped celery |
| ¼ | cup chopped green pepper |
| | Crisp salad greens |
| 1 | drop red food coloring |
| ⅓ | cup sour cream |
| 2 | tablespoons cranberry jelly |
| 1½ | tablespoons reserved peach syrup |

1. Drain canned peach halves reserving syrup, and set aside.
2. Blend cream cheese, mayonnaise, horse-radish and salt in a bowl.
3. Thoroughly mix in almonds, celery and green pepper.
4. Fill peach cavities with cheese mixture and press two peach halves together to make a whole peach. Chill if time allows.
5. Arrange peaches on large plate of salad greens.
6. Dilute red food coloring with water.
7. Gently brush color on top of each peach.
8. Blend together sour cream, cranberry jelly and peach syrup.
9. Serve with peaches.

*4 servings*
*25 min.*

**Pear Blush Salad:** Follow recipe for Peach Blush Salad. Substitute **canned pears** and **syrup** for peaches and syrup. Accompany each pear with a **maraschino cherry,** cut in eighths from stem end almost to base.

*25 min.*

**Apricot Salad:** Follow recipe for Peach Blush Salad. Substitute 16 **canned apricot halves** and **syrup** for peaches and syrup. Omit food coloring. Allow two whole apricots for each serving.

*25 min.*

# Individual Chicken Salads

⅓  cup French Dressing I
(one-half recipe, page 56)
4  large, firm tomatoes
1  cup (about 3 stalks) thinly
sliced celery
1  6-oz. can (about ¾ cup)
cubed, boned chicken
½  cup (about 2 oz.) diced
Swiss cheese
¼  cup chopped green pepper
¼  cup (about 1½ oz.) coarsely chopped, salted,
toasted (page 69) almonds
¼  teaspoon salt
⅛  teaspoon pepper
Blender Mayonnaise (page
56)

1. Prepare French Dressing and set aside.
2. For Tomato Shells—Rinse tomatoes and cut off tops.
3. Remove pulp from tomatoes with a spoon. Invert tomato shells and set aside to drain. Chill tomato shells in refrigerator until just before serving.
4. For Chicken Salad—Combine in a large bowl celery, chicken, Swiss cheese and green pepper.
5. Toss lightly with French Dressing I. Chill in refrigerator until ready to serve.
6. Set out almonds.
7. To Assemble—Sprinkle inside of tomatoes with a mixture of salt and pepper.
8. Drain salad mixture and blend in nuts. Lightly fill tomato shell.
9. Serve with Blender Mayonnaise.
10. Garnish with pitted and sliced ripe olives.

*4 servings*
*30 min.*

**Chicken Salad Bowl:** Follow recipe for Individual Chicken Salads. Omit tomato shells. Toss ¼ cup chopped **pimiento** and 4 sliced **Hard-Cooked Eggs** with remaining ingredients. To serve, lightly pile mixture in a salad bowl. Garnish with **water cress** or **parsley.**

*25 min.*

**Chicken-Waldorf Salad:** Follow recipe for Individual Chicken Salads. Omit tomato shells. Decrease celery to ½ cup. Wash, quarter, core and dice 1 medium-size **apple** (about 1 cup, diced). Substitute **walnuts** for almonds. Lightly toss with remaining ingredients. To serve, lightly pile into **lettuce cups.**

*25 min.*

**Individual Fish Salads:** Follow recipe for Individual Chicken Salads. Substitute for chicken, 1 cup (7- to 7¾-oz. can drained) flaked **tuna** or **salmon.** Substitute ¼ cup chopped **cucumber** for green pepper.

*25 min.*

# Kidney Bean Salad

4  Hard-Cooked Eggs
1  16-oz. can kidney beans
(about 2 cups, drained)
⅓  cup coarsely chopped
sweet pickle
¼  cup finely chopped onion
3  tablespoons sweet pickle
liquid or French Dressing
II (page 56)
½  cup Blender Mayonnaise
(page 56)
1  tablespoon pickle liquid

1. Prepare and dice eggs.
2. Meanwhile, drain contents of can kidney beans (discarding liquid).
3. Toss lightly with diced eggs and sweet pickle, onion and sweet pickle liquid.
4. Blend together mayonnaise and pickle liquid.
5. Pour over salad mixture and toss lightly to coat vegetables. Chill if time allows.
6. Serve in crisp lettuce cups.

*4 servings*
*30 min.*

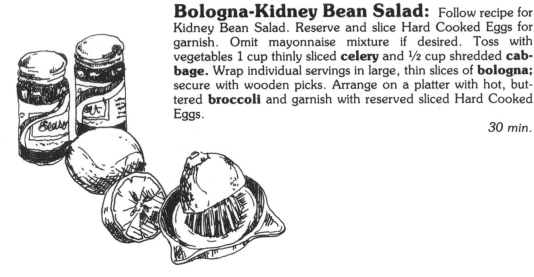

**Bologna-Kidney Bean Salad:** Follow recipe for Kidney Bean Salad. Reserve and slice Hard Cooked Eggs for garnish. Omit mayonnaise mixture if desired. Toss with vegetables 1 cup thinly sliced **celery** and ½ cup shredded **cabbage.** Wrap individual servings in large, thin slices of **bologna;** secure with wooden picks. Arrange on a platter with hot, buttered **broccoli** and garnish with reserved sliced Hard Cooked Eggs.

*30 min.*

# Sunshine Slaw

| | |
|---|---|
| ¾ | **lb. cabbage (about 3 cups, shredded)** |
| ½ | **lb. carrots, pared or scraped (about 1¼ cups, shredded)** |
| ¼ | **cup lemon juice** |
| 2 | **treaspoons grated onion** |
| ½ | **cup undiluted evaporated milk** |
| 2 | **tablespoons sugar** |
| 1 | **teaspoon salt** |
| ⅛ | **teaspoon pepper** |

1. Wash, shred, toss together cabbage and carrots and set aside in a large bowl.
2. Add lemon juice and onion into milk gradually, stirring constantly.
3. Stir in sugar, salt and pepper.
4. Pour over cabbage mixture and toss to coat cabbage and carrots well. Chill in refrigerator; serve on salad greens if desired.

*6 servings*
*20 min.*

**Cabbage Slaw:** Follow recipe for Sunshine Slaw. Omit carrots. Toss with **green pepper strips.**

*20 min.*

**Red 'n' Green Slaw:** Follow recipe for Sunshine Slaw. Substitute ¼ lb. (about 1 cup, shredded) **red cabbage** for carrots. Drain 9-oz. can **pineapple tidbits** (about ⅔ cup, drained); toss with cabbage.

*20 min.*

**Apple Slaw:** Follow recipe for Sunshine Slaw. Omit carrots. Wash quarter, core and thinly slice 3 red **apples;** toss with cabbage. Add 1 tablespoon **celery seed** with the seasonings.

*20 min.*

**Peanut Slaw:** Follow recipe for Sunshine Slaw. Decrease salt to ½ teaspoon. Just before serving, add ½ cup (about 3 oz.) coarsely chopped, **salted peanuts;** toss lightly.

*20 min.*

# Blossom Salad

4  oranges
1  9-oz. can pineapple tidbits
   (about ⅔ cup, drained)
1  banana with brown-flecked
   peel
1  cup (½ lb.) cottage cheese
2  tablespoons reserved
   pineapple syrup
   Sprigs of mint, water cress
   or parsley

1. Wash oranges.
2. Beginning at top, make 6 equally spaced cuts through orange peel to pulp; slit to within an inch of base. Pull each piece of peel away from pulp, forming 6 petals attached at base. Carefully pull fruit from base. Remove white membrane from fruit. Cut fruit into sections and set aside.
3. Set aside to drain, reserving syrup, contents of can pineapple tidbits.
4. Peel banana quarter lengthwise and dice.
5. Lightly toss orange sections, pineapple tidbits and diced banana together. Fill orange peel shells with fruit mixture.
6. Blend together cottage cheese and reserved pineapple syrup.
7. Spoon onto fruit. Top salads with sprigs of mint, water cress or parsley.
8. Serve on crisp salad greens.

*4 servings*
*30 min.*

**Lotus Luncheon Salad:** Follow recipe for Blossom Salad. Substitute **grapefruit** for oranges. Cut fruit sections into halves. Cut 6 **maraschino cherries** into quarters and toss with fruit.

*30 min.*

# Mint Apples

6  medium-size (2 lbs.) apples
2  cups sugar
1  cup water
¼  teaspoon green food coloring
5  drops peppermint extract

1. Wash apples and set aside.
2. Combine sugar and water in a deep saucepan and bring to boiling, stirring until sugar is dissolved.
3. Meanwhile, core and pare (leaving whole) only as many apples as will fit uncrowded in the saucepan.
4. Stir into syrup green food coloring and peppermint extract.
5. Add apples to syrup; cover and cook slowly just until tender (about 15 min.). Turn carefully several times to obtain an even color. With a slotted spoon, carefully remove apples from syrup; allow excess syrup to drain into saucepan. Core, pare and repeat cooking process for any remaining apples.
6. Garnish with mint leaves and serve warm or chilled with meat.

*6 servings*
*20 min.*

**Mint Apple Salad:** Follow recipe for Mint Apples. Chill apples in refrigerator. Fill core hole with a mixture of softened **cream cheese** and chopped **nuts**. Serve on crisp **lettuce leaves**.

# Dairyland Salad Dressing

1    cup (½ lb.) cream-style cottage cheese
½    cup thick sour cream
2    teaspoons Worcestershire sauce
¼    teaspoon salt
2    drops Tabasco
½    cup (about 2 oz.) crumbled Blue cheese
2    tablespoons minced onion
2    tablespoons coarsely chopped pimiento

1. Put into a bowl cottage cheese, sour cream, Worcestershire sauce, salt and Tabasco.
2. Beat with rotary beater until well blended. Add Blue cheese, onion and pimiento and mix thoroughly.

*About 2 cups salad dressing*
*15 min.*

# French Dressing I

1    tablespoon sugar
¼    teaspoon salt
¼    teaspoon paprika
¼    teaspoon dry mustard
6    tablespoons salad oil
¼    cup lemon juice

1. Blend well sugar, salt, paprika and dry mustard.
2. Put salad oil and lemon juice into a screw-top jar.
3. Cover jar tightly and shake vigorously to blend well. Store in same jar in refrigerator.
4. Before serving, beat or shake vigorously.

*About ⅔ cup dressing*
*10 min.*

**French Dressing II:** Follow recipe for French Dressing I. Increase paprika to ½ teaspoon. Omit lemon juice. Add 2 tablespoons **wine vinegar** with salad oil.

*10 min.*

# Blender Mayonnaise

1    egg, unbeaten
2    tablespoons vinegar or lemon juice
¼    teaspoon salt
¼    teaspoon sugar
¼    teaspoon dry mustard
¼    teaspoon paprika
3    drops Tabasco
¾    cup salad oil

1. Put egg, vinegar or lemon juice, salt, sugar, dry mustard, paprika and Tabasco into blender container in order.
2. Cover, turn on motor and blend thoroughly. Continue blending while pouring salad oil very slowly into center of ingredients.
3. Add oil just until it begins to layer on surface; mayonnaise then will be proper consistency. (If mayonnaise separates because oil is added too rapidly, beat it slowly and thoroughly into 1 egg yolk.)
4. Store covered in refrigerator.

*About 1 cup mayonnaise*
*10 min.*

# Shaker Salad Dressing

| | |
|---|---|
| ⅔ | cup (one-half 14-oz. can) sweetened condensed milk |
| ¼ | cup salad oil |
| 2 | tablespoons vinegar or lemon juice |
| ½ | teaspoon salt |
| ½ | teaspoon prepared mustard |

1. Measure into a 1-pt. screw-top jar condensed milk, salad oil, salt and prepared mustard.
2. Cover tightly and shake vigorously 1 min., or until well blended. Store covered in same jar in refrigerator.

*About 1 cup dressing*
*5 min.*

# Shades o' Green Salad

| | |
|---|---|
| ⅓ | cup French Dressing I (one-half recipe, page 56) |
| 3 | cups spinach (see Gourmet Spinach, page 50) |
| ½ | head lettuce |
| 4 | stalks pascal celery |
| ½ | green pepper |
| 1 | small cucumber, washed |
| 2 | tablespoons chopped chives |
| 1 | avocado |
| 6 | green olives |

1. Prepare French Dressing and set aside.
2. Wash spinach and set aside to drain thoroughly.
3. Rinse lettuce, discard bruised leaves and pat dry with a clean towel or absorbent paper.
4. Tear into bite-size pieces and set aside in a large bowl.
5. Coarsely chop or dice celery, pepper and cucumber.
6. Add chives to lettuce and toss lightly with French Dressing.
7. Arrange individual portions of salad on beds of spinach.
8. Rinse avocado, cut into halves, pit, peel and slice.
9. Pit and slice olives.
10. Garnish salads with avocado and olive slices.

*6 servings*
*30 min.*

# Avocados Stuffed with Cauliflower Salad

| | |
|---|---|
| 2 | cups very small, crisp raw cauliflowerets |
| 1 | cup cooked green peas |
| ½ | cup sliced ripe olives |
| ¼ | cup chopped pimento |
| ¼ | cup chopped onion |
| | Oil and Vinegar Dressing |
| | Salt to taste |
| 6 | small lettuce leaves |
| 3 | large ripe avocados |
| | Lemon wedges |

1. Combine all ingredients, except lettuce, avocados, and lemon wedges; stir gently until evenly mixed and coated with dressing.
2. Refrigerate at least 1 hour before serving.
3. When ready to serve, peel, halve, and remove pits from avocados. Place a lettuce leaf on each serving plate; top with avocado half filled with a mound of cauliflower salad. Serve with **lemon wedges.**

*6 servings*
*20 min.*

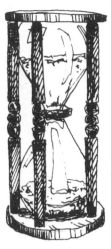
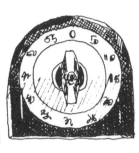

# SAUCES

## Fresh Cranberry Sauce

½ cup sugar
½ cup water
1 1-in. piece stick cinnamon
1 cup (about ¼ lb.) cranberries, washed and sorted

1. Combine sugar, water and cinnamon in a saucepan and heat to boiling.
2. Boil 5 min. Add cranberries.
3. Continue to boil uncovered without stirring about 5 min., or until skins of cranberries pop open. Cool and remove stick cinnamon.
4. Serve with meat or poultry.

*About 1 cup sauce*
*18 min.*

## Quick Cheese Sauce

½ lb. process Cheddar cheese
¼ cup milk
1½ teaspoons Worcestershire sauce
1 teaspoon prepared mustard

1. Melt Cheddar cheese in double boiler top over simmering water.
2. Add gradually, stirring until smooth, a mixture of milk, Worcestershire sauce and prepared mustard.

*About 1½ cups sauce*
*15 min.*

## Medium White Sauce

2 tablespoons butter or margarine
2 tablespoons all-purpose flour
¼ teaspoon salt
Few grains pepper
1 cup milk

1. Melt butter or margarine in a saucepan over low heat.
2. Blend in flour, salt and pepper.
3. Heat until mixture bubbles. Remove from heat. Add milk gradually.
4. Cook rapidly, stirring constantly, until sauce thickens. Cook 1 to 2 min. longer.
5. Use for gravies and creamed mixtures.

*About 1 cup sauce*
*10 min.*

*Note:* Quick Chicken Broth may be substituted for the milk.

### Thick White Sauce:
Follow recipe for Medium White Sauce. Use 3 to 4 tablespoons flour and 3 to 4 tablespoons butter or margarine. Use in preparation of souffles and croquettes.

*10 min.*

### Thin White Sauce:
Follow recipe for Medium White Sauce. Use 1 tablespoon flour and 1 tablespoon butter or margarine. Use as a base for cream soups. For a rich cream soup, substitute cream for milk.

*10 min.*

### Mock Hollandaise Sauce:
Follow recipe for Medium White Sauce using a double boiler top instead of a saucepan. When sauce is thickened, vigorously stir about 3 tablespoons of hot mixture into 2 **egg yolk,** slightly beaten. Return to sauce and cook over simmering water 3 to 5 min. Stir slowly to keep mixture cooking evenly. Stir in 1 tablespoon **lemon juice** and 2 tablespoons **butter** or **margarine.**

*15 min.*

### Tomato Sauce:
Follow recipe for Medium White Sauce. Cook 1 tablespoon finely chopped **onion** in the butter before adding flour mixture. Substitute **tomato juice** for milk. Blend in 1 teaspoon **Worcestershire sauce** with tomato juice.

*12 min.*

### Cheese Sauce:
Follow recipe for Medium White Sauce. Blend in ¼ teaspoon **dry mustard** and a few grains **cayenne pepper** with flour and seasonings. Cool sauce slightly. Add all at one time, ¼ cup (1 oz.) grated **Parmesan,** sharp **Cheddar** or **Swiss cheese.** Heat slowly, stirring constantly, until cheese is melted.

*20 min.*

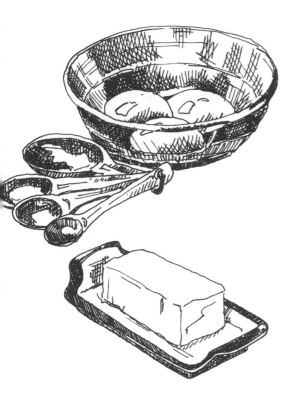

# Mustard Sauce

| | |
|---|---|
| 1 | cup cream or undiluted evaporated milk |
| ¼ | cup sugar |
| 2 | tablespoons dry mustard |
| 2 | teaspoons cornstarch |
| ½ | teaspoon salt |
| 1 | egg yolk, slightly beaten |
| ¼ | cup vinegar |

1. Set out cream or undiluted evaporated milk.
2. Scald ¾ cup of the cream in top of double boiler. Set remaining ¼ cup aside.
3. Sift together sugar, dry mustard, cornstarch and salt into a small saucepan.
4. Blend in the ¼ cup reserved cream or undiluted evaporated milk. Add gradually and stir in the scalded cream or milk.
5. Stirring gently and constantly, bring cornstarch mixture rapidly to boiling over direct heat and cook for 3 min.
6. Wash double boiler top to remove scum.
7. Pour mixture into double boiler top and place over simmering water. Cover and cook 10 to 12 min., stirring occasionally. Remove cover and vigorously stir about 3 tablespoons of hot mixture into egg yolk.
8. Immediately blend into mixture in double boiler. Cook over simmering water 3 to 5 min. Stir slowly to keep mixture cooking evenly. Remove from heat. Add vinegar gradually and stir.
9. Serve sauce hot with vegetables or meat.

*About 1¼ cups sauce*
*25 min.*

# Hollandaise Sauce

2    **egg yolks**
2    **tablespoons cream**
¼    **teaspoon salt**
     **Few grains cayenne pepper**
2    **tablespoons lemon juice**
     **or tarragon vinegar**
½    **cup butter or margarine**

1. Set out a small double boiler.
2. In the top of the double boiler, beat egg yolks and cream with a whisk beater until thickened and light colored.
3. Blend in salt and cayenne pepper.
4. Place top of double boiler over simmering water. (Bottom of double boiler top should not touch water.)
5. Add lemon juice or tarragon vinegar gradually, while beating constantly.
6. Cook over low heat, beating constantly with the whisk beater until sauce is the consistency of thick cream. Remove double boiler from heat, leaving top in place. Beating constantly, add butter or margarine to egg yolk mixture, ½ teaspoon at a time.
7. Beat with whisk beater until butter or margarine is thoroughly blended into mixture.
8. Serve hot over eggs, cooked vegetables or fish.
9. If necessary, sauce may be kept warm 15 min to 30 min. by setting it over hot water. Stir occasionally. Cover tightly.

*About 1 cup sauce*
*20 min.*

# Fish Sauce Supreme

½    **cup mayonnaise**
¼    **cup pickle relish**
2    **tablespoons chopped parsley**
1    **tablespoon lemon juice**
1    **teaspoon prepared horse-radish**
¼    **teaspoon salt**
2    **drops Tabasco**

1. Blend in a bowl mayonnaise, pickle relish, parsley, lemon juice, horse-radish, salt and Tabasco.
2. Put into refrigerator to chill and allow flavors to blend.

*About 1 cup sauce*
*5 min.*

# Maitre d' Hotel Butter

½    **cup softened butter**
2    **tablespoons lemon juice**
2    **teaspoons chopped parsley**
¼    **teaspoon salt**
⅛    **teaspoon pepper**

1. Cream thoroughly butter, lemon juice, parsley, salt and pepper.
2. Spread butter over broiled meat, fish and poultry just before serving.

*About ½ cup Maitre d'Hotel Butter*
*5 min.*

# Lemon Sauce

1½   **tablespoons butter or margarine**
2   **tablespoons all-purpose flour**
½   **teaspoon salt**
⅛   **teaspoon pepper**
¾   **cup boiling water**
¾   **cup undiluted evaporated milk**
2   **egg yolks, slightly beaten**
¼   **cup lemon juice**

1. Melt butter or margarine in a saucepan over low heat.
2. Blend in flour, salt and pepper.
3. Heat, stirring constantly, until mixture bubbles. Remove saucepan from heat. Add water and evaporated milk gradually stirring well after each addition.
4. Return to heat and bring rapidly to boiling, stirring constantly; cook 1 to 2 min. longer.
5. Vigorously stir about 3 tablespoons of hot mixture into egg yolks.
6. Immediately blend into mixture in saucepan. Continue to stir and cook 2 to 3 min. Stir in lemon juice.
7. Serve hot with fish.

*About 1¾ cups sauce*
*20 min.*

# DESSERTS

## Date-Vanilla Cream

⅓    **lb. pitted dates (about 1 cup, chopped)**
1¾    **cups milk**
⅔    **cup sugar**
3    **tablespoons cornstarch**
¼    **teaspoon salt**
¼    **cup cold milk**
3    **egg yolks, slightly beaten**
3    **tablespoons butter**
2    **teaspoons vanilla extract**

1. Chop dates and set aside.
2. Scald milk in double boiler top.
3. Meanwhile, sift sugar, cornstarch and salt together into a saucepan.
4. Stir in milk.
5. Gradually add scalded milk, stirring constantly.
6. Stirring gently and constantly, bring mixture rapidly to boiling over direct heat. Cook the mixture 3 min.
7. Wash double boiler top to remove scum.
8. Pour mixture into double boiler top; place over simmering water. Cover and cook about 12 min., stirring three or four times. Vigorously stir about 3 tablespoons hot mixture into egg yolks.
9. Immediately blend into mixture in double boiler. Cook over simmering water 3 to 5 min.; stir slowly to keep mixture cooking evenly. Remove from heat and stir in the chopped dates, butter and vanilla extract.
10. Cool slightly.
11. Pour into serving dishes. Cover and chill in refrigerator until ready to serve.
12. Top with Sweetened Whipped Cream.

*6 servings*
*30 min.*

**Maple Cream Pudding:** Follow recipe for Date-Vanilla Cream. Substitute 1 cup **maple syrup** for sugar and heat with milk. Omit dates and vanilla extract. Top servings with ⅓ cup (about 2 oz.) coarsely chopped **hazelnuts**.

*30 min.*

# Minted Pears

8  medium-size canned pear halves (17-oz. can)
1  cup reserved pear syrup
2  tablespoons lemon juice
1  teaspoon grated lemon peel
8  chocolate-coated mint patties

1. Set out 11x7x1½-in. baking dish.
2. Drain canned pear halves reserving syrup.
3. Place in the baking dish, cut-side up.
4. Mix pear syrup, lemon juice, and lemon peel in a bowl.
5. Pour over pears. Place mint patties in core cavities.
6. Bake at 375°F 8 to 10 min., or until patties are softened.
7. Serve warm with the syrup.

*4 servings*
*15 min.*

**Meringue Pear Mounds:** Follow recipe for Minted Pears. While Minted Pears are baking, prepare **Meringue** (see Jiffy Lemon Pie, page 65). Spoon into mounds over softened patties. Return to oven and bake 8 to 10 min. longer, or until meringue is lightly browned. Serve hot.

*25 min.*

**Holiday Pears:** Follow recipe for Minted Pears. Substitute ½ cup **currant** or **cranberry jelly** for mint patties. Bake until jelly melts. Beat 1 pkg. (3 oz.) **cream cheese** with 3 tablespoons **milk** until light and fluffy. Spoon onto each serving.

*15 min.*

# Baked Spiced Peaches

1  29-oz. can peach halves
¼  cup reserved peach syrup
¼  cup firmly packed brown sugar
½  teaspoon cinnamon
¼  teaspoon nutmeg
¼  cup coarsely crushed corn flakes
2  tablespoons finely chopped pecans
2  tablespoons butter or margarine melted

1. Set out 4 small individual baking dishes or a shallow baking dish.
2. Drain can peach halves reserving syrup.
3. Arrange peaches, cut-side up, in baking dishes. Pour over peaches a mixture of peach syrup, brown sugar, cinnamon and nutmeg.
4. Bake at 375°F 10 min., basting two or three times. Remove from oven. Increase oven temperature to 400°F. Sprinkle over peaches a mixture of corn flakes, pecans and butter or margarine.
5. Return to oven and bake 5 min. longer.
6. Serve peaches warm with cream.

*4 servings*
*25 min.*

# Graham Cracker Crumb Crust

| | |
|---|---|
| 15 | graham crackers |
| ¼ | cup sugar |
| ⅛ | teaspoon salt |
| ¼ | cup softened butter or margarine |

1. Set out a 9-in. pie pan.
2. Place graham crackers on a long length of heavy waxed paper.
3. Loosely fold paper around crackers, tucking under open ends. With rolling pin, gently crush crackers to make fine crumbs (about 1¼ cups). Turn crumbs into a bowl. Stir in sugar and salt.
4. Using a fork or pastry blender, evenly cut in ¼ cup softened butter or margarine.
5. Press crumb mixture evenly over bottom and sides of pie pan; press with spoon until firm.
6. Bake at 375°F 8 min.

*One 9-in. pie shell*
*20 min.*

**Nut Crumb Crust:** Follow recipe for Graham Cracker Crumb Crust. Decrease graham cracker crumbs to 1 cup and mix in ⅓ cup finely chopped **nuts.**

*25 min.*

**Graham Cracker Crumb Tart Shells:** Follow recipe for Graham Cracker Crumb Crust. Use 8 muffin pan wells. Line with paper baking cups. Press mixture into paper cups. Bake at 375°F 6 min. Cool. Carefully remove paper baking cups from shells.

*25 min.*

**Cookie Crumb Crust:** Follow recipe for Graham Cracker Crumb Crust. Substitute **gingersnaps, vanilla, lemon** or **chocolate wafers** (about twenty-four 2 ⅛-in. cookies) for graham crackers. Omit sugar.
Bake chocolate crumb shell at 325°F 10 min.

*20 min.*

# Luscious Blueberry Pie

| | |
|---|---|
| 1 | baked 9-in. pie shell |
| 2 | 16-oz. cans blueberries (about 2½ cups, drained) |
| 3 | tablespoons cornstarch |
| 1 | cup reserved blueberry syrup |
| 6 | tablespoons sugar |
| 2 | tablespoons lemon juice |
| 1½ | tablespoons butter or margarine |
| ⅛ | teaspoon salt |

1. Set out pie shell.
2. Drain cans blueberries reserving syrup.
3. Set aside blueberries.
4. Combine cornstarch and blueberry syrup in a saucepan and thoroughly blend together.
5. Stirring constantly, bring rapidly to boiling. Continue stirring and cooking until thick and clear. Stir in sugar.
6. Remove from heat and mix in lemon juice, butter or margarine and salt.
7. Gently mix in the blueberries. Set pan in bowl of ice and water to chill quickly. Pour cooled filling into pie shell.
8. Serve with ice cream.

*About 6 servings*
*30 min.*

**Muffins and Biscuits 19–22**

**Cherry Pie:** Follow recipe for Luscious Blueberry Pie. Substitute pitted **tart red cherries** for blueberries; if necessary, add water to cherry liquid. Increase sugar to ¾ cup. Substitute ¼ teaspoon **almond extract** for lemon juice. Blend in one or more drops **red food coloring** with the almond extract.

*30 min.*

# Glazed Strawberry Pie

| | |
|---|---|
| 1 | baked 9-in. pie shell |
| 1 | qt. strawberries, rinsed (discarding imperfect berries) and hulled |
| ¼ | cup plus 2 tablespoons sugar |
| 1½ | tablespoons cornstarch |
| ¼ | cup plus 2 tablespoons water |
| 1 | teaspoon lemon juice |
| 4 | drops red food coloring |
| 1 | pkg. (3 oz.) cream cheese |
| 1 | tablespoon orange juice |
| | Sweetened Whipped Cream (page 66) |

1. Set out pie shell and strawberries.
2. Set aside 2 cups whole berries. Crush remaining berries with fork and set aside.
3. Mix sugar, cornstarch and water in a saucepan in order.
4. Stirring gently and constantly, bring rapidly to boiling and cook for 3 min., or until mixture is clear. Stir in the crushed berries and blend in lemon juice and food coloring.
5. Cool mixture slightly with pan set in bowl of ice and water. Cover and set aside.
6. Beat together cream cheese and orange juice until blended.
7. Spread over bottom of pie shell; cover with whole berries. Pour cooled strawberry mixture over berries. Chill in refrigerator.
8. Top with Sweetened Whipped Cream.

*About 6 servings*
*30 min.*

# Jiffy Lemon Pie

| | |
|---|---|
| 1 | baked 8-in. pie shell |
| 1¼ | cups (14-oz. can) sweetened condensed milk |
| ⅔ | cup lemon juice |
| 1½ | teaspoons grated lemon peel |
| 2 | egg yolks, slightly beaten |
| 2 | egg whites |
| ⅛ | teaspoon salt |
| ¼ | cup sugar |

1. Set out pie shell.
2. Blend thoroughly condensed milk, lemon juice, lemon peel and egg yolks.
3. Pour into shell and set aside.
4. For Meringue—Beat egg whites and salt until frothy.
5. Add sugar gradually, beating well after each addition.
6. Beat until rounded peaks are formed and egg whites do not slide when bowl is partially inverted. Pile meringue lightly onto filling being sure to seal meringue to crust.
7. Bake at 350°F 10 to 12 min., or until meringue is delicately browned. Set aside to cool until ready to serve.

*About 6 servings*
*30 min.*

**Jiffy Lime Pie:** Follow recipe for Jiffy Lemon Pie. Substitute **lime peel** and ⅔ cup **lime juice** for lemon; add 1 or 2 drops **green food coloring**.

*30 min.*

# Little Tarts

1. Set out small baked pastry or crumb tart shells; fill with any of the following fillings.

*8 tarts*

# Lemon Curd Filling

½   **cup blueberries**
2   **eggs, slightly beaten**
½   **cup sugar**
⅓   **cup butter or margarine**
¼   **cup lemon juice**
1   **tablespoon grated lemon peel**

1. Rinse blueberries discard imperfect berries, drain and set aside.
2. Mix together eggs, sugar, butter or margarine, lemon juice and lemon peel in top of double boiler.
3. Cook over simmering water, stirring constantly, until mixture is thickened. Set pan in bowl of ice and water to chill quickly.
4. Fill tart shells with cooled mixture; top with blueberries.

*30 min.*

# Sweetened Whipped Cream

1   **cup chilled whipping cream**
3   **tablespoons confectioners' sugar**
1   **teaspoon vanilla extract**

1. Beat whipping cream in chilled bowl with chilled rotary beater.
2. Beat until cream stands in peaks when beater is slowly lifted upright. Beat confectioners' sugar and vanilla extract into whipped cream with final few strokes.
3. For a Pleasing Variation—Mix with sugar and beat in with final few strokes 1 teaspoon **cinnamon,** ½ teaspoon **nutmeg** and ⅛ teaspoon **cloves.** Or fold in about 1 cup crushed **peanut brittle** or 1 cup chopped **nuts.**

*20 min.*

# Cream Fillings

Prepare any of the following fillings:
**Jiffy Lemon or Lime Pie (page 65).**
**Date-Vanilla Cream (page 62).**
**Maple Cream Pudding (page 62).**

*30 min.*

# Soft Custard

**2** cups milk
**4** egg yolks
**¼** cup sugar
**⅛** teaspoon salt
**2** teaspoons vanilla extract

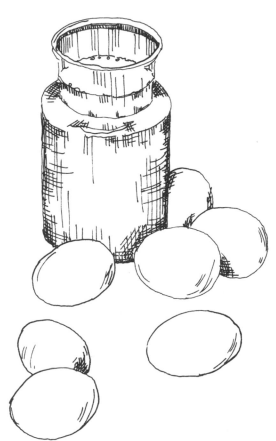

1. Scald milk in top of double boiler.
2. Meanwhile, beat egg yolks slightly.
3. Blend in sugar and salt.
4. Gradually stir hot milk into eggs. Strain and return to double boiler. Cook over simmering water, stirring constantly and rapidly until mixture coats a silver spoon. Remove from heat at once. Blend in vanilla extract.
5. Pour immediately into 6 sherbet glasses. Set aside to cool until lukewarm and immediately chill in refrigerator.
6. Sprinkle with chopped nuts if desired.

*6 servings*
*25 min.*

**Custard with Brittle:** Follow recipe for Soft Custard. Crush ½ cup **nut brittle.** Spoon ¼ cup into sherbet glasses. Pour in Soft Custard and top with the remaining ¼ cup crushed nut brittle.

*25 min.*

**Minty Custard:** Follow recipe for Soft Custard. Just before serving, prepare **Sweetened Whipped Cream** (one-half recipe, page 66). Add 1 or 2 drops **peppermint extract** with vanilla extract. Alternate layers of custard and whipped cream in sherbet glasses, ending with whipped cream.

*30 min.*

**Brownie Custard:** Follow recipe for Soft Custard. Put ½ cup **brownie crumbs** into sherbet glasses. Pour custard over crumbs. Sprinkle a few crumbs over the top.

*25 min.*

**Fruit Custard:** Follow recipe for Soft Custard. Pour custard over **orange sections** or well-drained **fruit.**

*25 min.*

**Date Custard:** Follow recipe for Soft Custard. Cut 8 pitted **dates** into slivers. Reserving a few date slivers for garnish, place remaining dates in sherbet glasses. Pour in Soft Custard; garnish servings with reserved dates.

*25 min.*

**Floating Island:** Follow recipe for Soft Custard. Beat 3 **egg whites** until frothy. Add ¼ teaspoon **salt** and ½ teaspoon **vanilla extract.** Gradually add 6 tablespoons **sugar,** beating well after each addition and continuing to beat until rounded peaks are formed. Drop by tablespoonfuls into simmering (not boiling) water. Cover. Cook about 5 min., or until set. Remove meringues and drain on absorbent paper. Float on chilled Soft Custard just before serving.

*30 min.*

## Ice Cream Specialties

Add to purchased ice cream: **mincemeat;** crushed **berries;** chopped **nuts;** crushed hard candies such as **lemon drops** or **peppermints.** or any **nut-brittle candies.**

Mash ice cream with spoon or blending fork; beat until smooth. Blend in one of the above and turn into freezing tray. Chill in freezing compartment of refrigerator until firm.

## Sauces For Ice Cream

Pour over purchased ice cream any of the following sauces:

*Soft Custard* (page 67).

*Caramel Sauce*—Heat over simmering water 1/2 lb. vanilla caramels and 1/3 cup milk; stir.

*Fudge Sauce*—Heat in top of double boiler over simmering water until chocolate is melted, 2 sq. (2 oz.) **chocolate,** 2 tablespoons **butter** or **margarine** and 2/3 cup hot **water.** Add 1 3/4 cups **sugar,** 1/4 cup **light corn syrup** and 1/4 teaspoon **salt;** stir until sugar is dissolved. Bring mixture just to boiling over direct heat, stirring constantly. Simmer over low heat 5 min. Stir in 1 teaspoon **vanilla extract.** Serve hot.

*About 1 1/2 cups sauce*

For a marbled sauce, cut 8 **marshmallows** into pieces and simmer with fudge mixture; stir slightly.

*Chocolate Sauce*—Heat in double boiler top over simmering water until chocolate is melted, 1/2 cup **milk** and 1 pkg. (6 oz.) **semi-sweet chocolate pieces.** Stir in 1/4 teaspoon **vanilla extract** and 1/4 teaspoon **almond** or **peppermint extract.**

*About 1 cup sauce*

*Butterscotch Sauce*—Combine and bring to boiling in a heavy saucepan, 1 cup firmly packed **brown sugar,** 1 cup **light corn syrup,** 1/3 cup **cream,** 1/3 cup **water** and 2 tablespoons **butter** or **margarine;** stir only until sugar is dissolved. Cook to 230°F, or until syrup forms a soft ball in very cold water; ball flattens when removed from water.

*About 1 1/2 cups sauce*

*Coffee Sauces*—Mix in a saucepan 1/3 cup **sugar,** 1 tablespoon **cornstarch** and 1/8 teaspoon **salt.** Gradually stir in 2/3 cup **cream** and 3/4 cup **double-**strength coffee beverage (page 10). Stirring constantly, bring to boiling over medium heat. Cover and simmer 3 min. Add 1/2 teaspoon **vanilla extract** and 1 tablespoon **butter** or **margarine.**

*About 1 1/2 cups sauce*

*Quick Coffee Sauce*—Follow recipe for Coffee Sauce, omitting coffee beverage. Mix 2 to 3 teaspoons **concentrated soluble coffee** in saucepan with dry ingredients. Increase cream to 1 1/2 cups.

*About 1 1/2 cups sauce*

*Red Cherry Sauce*—Mix in a saucepan 2/3 cup **sugar,** 2 tablespoons **cornstarch** and 1/8 teaspoon **salt.** Drain, reserving liquid, 1 16 oz. can pitted **tart red cherries** (yields about 1 1/2 cups cherries). Gradually stir in 1 1/2 cups reserved liquid. Stirring constantly, bring to boiling over medium heat. Cover and simmer 3 min. Add drained cherries, 1 tablespoon **butter** or **margarine** and 1/4 teaspoon **almond extract.**

*About 3 cups sauce*

*Raspberry Sauce*—Mix in a saucepan 1/3 cup **sugar,** 1 teaspoon **cornstarch** and 1/8 teaspoon **salt.** Mash 1 cup fresh **red raspberries.** Add gradually, stirring in, raspberries and 1/2 cup **currant jelly.** Stir constantly and bring to boiling over medium heat. Cover and simmer 3 min. Add 1/2 teaspoon **vanilla extract** and 1 tablespoon **butter** or **margarine.** Strain cooked sauce. Cool and serve with peach ice cream.

*About 1 1/2 cups sauce*

*Maraschino Sauce*—Mix in a saucepan 1/3 cup **sugar,** 1 1/2 tablespoons **cornstarch** and 1/8 teaspoon **salt.** Drain 8-oz. jar **maraschino cherries,** reserving syrup. Gradually stir in reserved syrup and 1 cup **water.** Stirring constantly, bring to boiling over medium heat. Cover; simmer 3 min. Stir in cherries, cut in halves.

*About 2 1/2 cups sauce*

## Toppers For Ice Cream

Top purchased ice cream with any of the following: shaved **maple sugar; maple syrup; honey; applesauce,** sprinkled with **cinnamon;** fresh **peaches; whipped cream,** flavored with **peppermint extract;** toasted **macaroon crumbs;** or:

*Chocolate Curls*—Pull **chocolate squares** across a shredder.

*Colored Coconut*—Place flaked, shredded or grated **coconut** on waxed paper and sprinkle with a mixture of a few drops each of **food coloring** and **water.** Toss well, dry and toast in a slow oven.

*Frozen Fruit*—Thaw partially.

*Sweetened Crushed Berries*—Rinse, discard imperfect berries and hull 1 qt. **strawberries.** Reserve ½ cup berries for garnish if desired.

Crush remaining berries slightly and sweeten with about 1 cup **sugar.** Cover and set in refrigerator to chill thoroughly. Gently mix fruit occasionally.

**Raspberries, blackberries** or **blueberries** may be substituted for strawberries.

*Blanched Almonds*—Bring to rapid boiling enough **water** to well cover shelled nuts. Drop in only about ½ cup **nuts.** Turn off heat and allow to remain in the water about 1 min. (Flavor of nuts is best maintained when in water the shortest possible time.) Drain or remove with fork or slotted spoon.

Place between folds of absorbent paper; pat dry. Gently squeeze nuts with fingers to remove skins. Place on absorbent paper to dry thoroughly. Frequently shift nuts to dry spots on paper. Repeat blanching process for larger amounts of nuts.

*Toasted Nuts*—Place **nuts** in a shallow baking dish or pie pan and brush lightly with **cooking oil.** Heat in oven at 350°F until delicately browned. Stir and turn occasionally. Or, add nuts to a heavy skillet in which **butter** (about 1 tablespoon per cup of nuts) has been melted. Brown nuts lightly, stirring constantly, over moderate heat.

*Salted Nuts*—Proceed as for Toasted Nuts. Drain the nuts on absorbent paper and sprinkle them with **salt.**

## Bakery Cakes at Home

### Frost Or Fill Cakes

*Prepare* **Quick Fudge Frosting** (page 70), **White Velvet Frosting** (page 71), **Toasted Pecan Frosting** (page 70), or **Lemon Curd Filling** (page 66).

*To Fill Cakes*—Spread frosting or filling over top of bottom layer. Cover with the other layer. Repeat procedure if more layers are used. If necessary, hold layers in position with wooden picks; remove when frosting is set.

*To Frost Cakes*—Frost sides first, working rapidly. See that frosting touches plate all around bottom leaving no gaps. Pile remaining frosting on top and spread lightly.

Top or fill cakes with firm **ice cream** and melted **semi-sweet chocolate**—serve promptly.

Fold mashed **bananas,** crushed **nut brittle** or grated **chocolate** into **Sweetened Whipped Cream** (page 66).

Fill a cake shell with **ice cream, custard** or flavored **whipped cream.** For cake shell, carefully cut a 1-in. layer from top of a cake; cut or scoop out center of cake, leaving at least a 1-in. thick shell. Pieces of cake from center may be folded into the custard or whipped cream. Top with layer cut from cake.

### Toppers For Cakes

Add distinction to a plain cake by giving it a baked or broiled topping; or dress up individual servings with quickly made sauces.

Try **Soft Custard** (page 67) with an added ½ teaspoon **sherry** or **rum extract; Fudge Sauce, Chocolate, Butterscotch, Coffee, Red Cherry Sauce** (page 68) or:

*Orange Sauce*—Combine in top of double boiler 2 **egg yolks,** slightly beaten, ⅓ cups **sugar** and ¼ cup **orange juice.** Cook over simmering water, stirring constantly, until thickened. Set pan in bowl of ice and water to chill quickly. Fold in 1 tablespoon grated **orange peel** and 1 cup **whipped cream.**

*About 1½ cups sauce*

**Bake-Quick Toppings:** Place cake on baking sheet and spread with Honey Topping or Meringue-Nut Topping.

Bake at 425°F 8 to 10 min.

*Honey Topping*—Mix ⅓ cup **honey,** 2 tablespoons softened **butter** or **margarine** and ½ cup **flaked coconut.**

*Meringue-Nut Topping*—Prepare **Meringue** (see Jiffy Lemon Pie, page 65) and spread over cake. Sprinkle with chopped **nuts.**

**Broil-Quick Toppings:** Place cake on broiler pan. Cover cake with Nut Topping or Coconut Topping.

Set temperature control of range at Broil.

Place broiler pan in broiler with top of cake 3 in.

from heat source; broil about 3 min., or until lightly toasted.

*Nut Topping* — Generously spread cake or cake slices with **butter** or **margarine.** Sprinkle with a mixture of **cinnamon, sugar** or **brown sugar,** and chopped **salted nuts.**

*Coconut Topping* — Cream 3 tablespoons **butter** or **margarine** with 2 tablespoons **peanut butter.** Mix in ⅓ cup firmly packed **brown sugar** and 2 tablespoons **cream;** spread over cake. Sprinkle with **flaked coconut.**

**Decorate with Confectioners' Sugar:** Place a lacy paper doily on top of cake and sift **confectioners' sugar** over doily; carefully remove doily from cake.

**Make A Party Dessert**
Use shortcut methods for old favorites.

*Cherry Upside-Down Cake* — Set out a heavy 10-in. skillet and its cover. Drain 1 16-oz. can pitted tart red cherries; reserve syrup, adding **water** to make 1 cup. Combine in skillet ⅓ cup **sugar** and 2½ tablespoons **cornstarch.** Gradually stir in liquid. Stirring constantly, bring to boiling over medium heat. Simmer 3 min. Add cherries, 1 tablespoon **butter** or **margarine** and ¼ teaspoon **lemon extract.**

Place in skillet on top of mixture 1 9-in. round **cake layer,** or cut a 1½-in. thick cake layer from a 9-in. tubed cake. Cover and cook over low heat about 5 min. Invert immediately onto serving plate. Let skillet rest over cake a few seconds so sauce will drain onto cake.

*Baked Alaska Loaf* — Cut a 1-in. thick layer from a **sponge cake** or **pound cake** and place on a wooden board or baking sheet covered with 2 sheets heavy paper; set aside. Prepare **Meringue** (see Jiffy Lemon Pie, double recipe, page 65; use ¾ cup sugar). Place 1 pt. firm purchased **ice cream** on cake; trim cake to within 1 in. of ice cream. Completely cover ice cream and cake with meringue.

Bake at 450°F 3 to 5 min., or until meringue is lightly browned. Serve immediately.

*4 servings*

# Toasted Pecan Frosting

| | |
|---|---|
| 1 | cup (about ¼ lb.) coarsely chopped pecans |
| ¼ | cup butter |
| ½ | cup cream |
| 1½ | teaspoons vanilla extract |
| ⅛ | teaspoon salt |
| 3 | cups sifted confectioners' sugar |

1. Stir pecans and butter constantly in skillet over medium heat until pecans are toasted.
2. Remove from heat. Stir in cream, vanilla extract, salt and confectioners' sugar in order.
3. Blend until smooth enough to spread onto cake.

*Enough to frost sides and top of one 8-or 9-in. square cake*
*20 min.*

# Quick Fudge Frosting

| | |
|---|---|
| 1 | pkg. (6 oz.) semi-sweet chocolate pieces |
| ⅔ | cup (one-half 14-oz. can) sweetened condensed milk |
| 1 | tablespoon water |

1. Heat chocolate pieces, condensed milk and water in top of double boiler.
2. Stir until chocolate is melted and mixture is smooth. Remove from heat; cool in pan of ice and water.

*Enough to frost sides and top of one 8-in. square cake*
*15 min.*

# White Velvet Frosting

¼ cup butter or margarine
1½ teaspoons vanilla extract
⅛ teaspoon salt
3 cups sifted confectioners' sugar
1 egg yolk
3 tablespoons milk or cream

1. Cream together butter or margarine, vanilla extract and salt until shortening is softened.
2. Add confectioners' sugar gradually, beating until smooth after each addition.
3. Blend in egg yolk.
4. Add milk or cream slowly to blended mixture.
5. Add only enough milk or cream to make frosting the consistency for spreading.

*Enough to frost sides and tops of two 8- or 9-in. round cake layers*
*10 min.*

**Brown Velvet Frosting:** Follow recipe for White Velvet Frosting. Melt and cool 2 sq. (2 oz.) **chocolate;** mix in after egg yolk addition.

*15 min.*

**Chocolate-Mocha Frosting:** Follow recipe for White Velvet Frosting. Decrease sugar to 2⅔ cups; sift with ⅓ cup **cocoa.** Substitute **double-strength coffee beverage** for the milk or cream.

*15 min.*

**Creamy Orange Frosting:** Follow recipe for White Velvet Frosting. Substitute **orange juice** for milk or cream. Add 2 or 3 drops **orange food coloring.** Sprinkle grated **orange peel** over top of frosted cake.

*10 min.*

# Date and Nut Roll

Creamy Orange Frosting (page 71; omit grated peel and food coloring)
2 8-oz. cans date and nut bread
Flaked coconut

1. Prepare Creamy Orange Frosting.
2. Remove contents from cans date and nut bread.
3. Split each into halves lengthwise. Spread cutsides with frosting and re-form rolls. Place bread end to end to form a long roll; frost sides and ends. Generously sprinkle with flaked coconut.
4. Garnish with maraschino cherries.

*8 to 10 servings*
*20 min.*

# Strawberry-Pear Flambee

2 packages (10 ounces each) frozen strawberries (thaw ahead of time)
1 cup sugar
6 tablespoons butter
½ cup orange juice
1½ teaspoons grated lemon peel
1 can (29 ounces) large pear halves, drained
⅓ cup cognac

1. Drain strawberries; reserve juice. Put berries through a sieve to puree. Add desired amount of reserved juice to sweeten and thin puree; set aside.
2. In cooking pan of a chafing dish, caramelize sugar with butter over medium heat. Stir in orange juice, lemon peel, and puree. Simmer sauce 1 to 2 minutes, stirring gently.
3. Place pears in sauce and roll in sauce until they are thoroughly heated and have a blush.
4. In a separate pan, heat cognac just until warm. Ignite the cognac and pour over the pears. Spoon the sauce over pears until the flames die out.
5. Serve the pears in dessert dishes with the sauce.

*4 servings*
*25 min.*

# BAKING MIXES

## All-in-One Biscuit Mix

| | |
|---|---|
| **8** | **cups sifted all-purpose flour** |
| **¼** | **cup baking powder** |
| **4** | **teaspoons salt** |
| **2** | **cups lard, hydrogenated vegetable shortening or all-purpose shortening** |

1. Sift flour, baking powder and salt together into a large mixing bowl.
2. Cut lard, hydrogenated vegetable shortening or all-purpose shortening into dry ingredients with pastry blender or two knives until mixture resembles coarse corn meal.
3. Store mix in tightly covered container in a cool place. (Biscuit mix made with lard should be stored in refrigerator.)

*About 12 cups biscuit mix*
*20 min.*

*Note:* Before measuring for use in recipe, lighten mix by tossing with fork.

## Rolled Biscuits

| | |
|---|---|
| **3** | **cups All-in-One Biscuit Mix (on this page)** |
| **⅔** | **cup milk** |
| | **Milk** |

1. Set out a baking sheet.
2. Measure biscuit mix into a mixing bowl.
3. Make a well in center of biscuit mix and add milk all at one time.
4. Stir with a fork until dough follows fork. Gently form dough into a ball. Turn onto lightly floured surface. To knead, fold opposite side of dough over toward you; press lightly with finger tips and turn dough quarter turn. Repeat 10 to 15 times.
5. Gently roll out dough from center to edge until about ½ in. thick. Cut dough with floured cutter or knife, using an even pressure to keep sides of biscuit straight. Place biscuits on baking sheet. Brush surfaces of biscuits with milk.
6. Bake at 450°F 10 to 15 min.

*About 18 2-in. biscuits*
*25 min.*

**Drop Biscuits:** Follow recipe for Rolled Biscuits. Increase milk to 1 cup. Omit kneading, rolling and cutting processes. Drop by spoonfuls onto baking sheet.

*23 min.*

**Applesauce Turnovers:** Follow recipe for Rolled Biscuits. Roll dough into a rectangle about ¼ in. thick; cut into 4-in. squares. Place 1 tablespoon thick sweetened **applesauce** in center of each square. Fold diagonally in half, pressing edges together.

Applesauce may be sweetened with **honey** or **sugar** and flavored with **cinnamon. Jam, marmalade, preserves** or **jelly** may be substituted for applesauce.

*25 min.*

**Peach Cobbler:** Drain contents of 1 17-oz. can sliced **peaches,** reserving syrup (about 1½ cups peaches, drained). Set aside.

Combine 2 tablespoons **sugar** with 1 tablespoon **cornstarch** in a saucepan. Add gradually, and stir in reserved peach syrup. Bring to boiling and cook about 1 min.

Add peaches, 1 tablespoon **butter** or **margarine** and ½ teaspoon **almond extract.**

Pour into shallow baking dish. Keep piping hot in oven while preparing one-half recipe **Drop Biscuits.** Add 1 tablespoon **sugar** to mix. Drop by spoonfuls over fruit mixture and bake.

*30 min.*

**Scones:** Follow recipe for Rolled Biscuits. Add 2 tablespoons **sugar** to biscuit mix. Decrease milk to ½ cup. Add 1 **egg,** well beaten, with milk. Cut biscuits into diamonds squares or triangles. Sprinkle with sugar after brushing with milk.

*25 min.*

**Quick Rolls:** Follow recipe for Rolled Biscuits. Fill and shape as **Cinnamon** or **Apple Rolls,** (page 20) **Orange Rolls** (page 21), and **Coconut Twists** (page 21).

*25 min.*

**Orange Tea Biscuits:** Follow recipe for Rolled Biscuits. Dip a loaf of **sugar** in **orange juice.** Press into top of each biscuit before baking. Sprinkle with grated **orange peel.**

*25 min.*

**Shortcakes:** Follow recipe for Rolled Biscuits. Add 1 tablespoon **sugar** to biscuit mix. Use 3-in. cutter to cut cakes. Split open when baked; spread with softened **butter** or **margarine.** Serve with **Sweetened Crushed Berries** (page 69) and **Sweetened Whipped Cream** (page 66).

*25 min.*

**Luncheon Meat Rolls:**   Follow recipe for Rolled Biscuits. Grease baking sheet. Roll dough into rectangle ¼ in. thick. Brush with mixture of 1 tablespoon softened **butter** or **margarine** and 2 teaspoons **prepared mustard.**
Spread dough with 1½ cups (12-oz. can) ground canned **luncheon meat.** Starting with long side of dough, roll up; pinch ends to seal. Cut into 1-in. slices and place on baking sheet. While rolls bake, heat contents of 2 16-oz. cans **French-style green beans.** Prepare 2 cups **Medium White Sauce** (double recipe, page 58). Drain beans; combine with sauce and 2 tablespoons diced **pimiento.** Serve sauce topped with meat rolls.

*8 servings*
*30 min.*

**Cheese Biscuits:**   Follow recipe for Rolled Biscuits. Blend ½ cup (2 oz.) grated **Cheddar cheese** into biscuit mix. Or, sprinkle grated **Parmesan cheese** over tops of biscuits before baking.

**Chive Biscuits:**   Follow recipe for Rolled Biscuits. Add ¼ cup finely chopped **chives** to biscuit mix.

# Perfect Pastry Mix

6   **cups sifted all-purpose flour**
1   **tablespoon salt**
2   **cups (1 lb.) lard, hydrogenated vegetable shortening or all-purpose shortening**

1. Sift together flour and salt into a large bowl.
2. Cut in lard, hydrogenated vegetable shortening or all-purpose shortening with pastry blender or two knives until pieces are size of small peas.
3. Store in covered bowl or container in refrigerator and use as needed. Will keep at least 1 month.

*About eight 8-in. or*
*six 9-in. pie shells*
*30 min.*

**How To Use Perfect Pastry Mix**
Before measuring for recipe, lighten mix by tossing with fork. Lightly pile mix into measuring cup. Level with straight-edge knife.

*For 1-Crust Pies* — Use 1 cup pastry mix with 2 to 3 tablespoons water for 8-in. pie shells. Use 1¼ cups mix with 2 to 3 tablespoons water for 9-in. pie shells.

*For 2-Crust Pies* — Use 2 cups pastry mix with 3 to 5 tablespoons water for 9-in. 2-crust pie.

*Note:* Two-crust pies require too long a baking period to be considered quick. Therefore, no recipes are included for 2-crust pies.

# Pastry for 1-Crust Pie

1¼ cups Perfect Pastry Mix
(page 74)
3 tablespoons cold water

1. Set out an 8-or 9-in. pie pan.
2. Measure pastry mix into a bowl.
3. Sprinkle cold water gradually over mixture, a teaspoon at a time.
4. Mix lightly with a fork after each addition. Add only enough water to hold pastry together. Work quickly; do not overhandle. Shape into a ball and flatten on a lightly floured surface.
5. (If dough is not to be used immediately, wrap in waxed paper, moisture-vaporproof material or aluminum foil and place in refrigerator.)
6. Roll dough in all directions from center to edge to about ⅛-in. thickness and about 1-in. larger than over-all size of pan. With knife or spatula, loosen pastry from surface wherever sticking occurs; lift pastry slightly and sprinkle flour underneath.
7. Loosen one-half of pastry from board with spatula and fold over other half. Loosen remaining part and fold in quarters. Gently lay pastry in pan and unfold, carefully fitting it to the pan so that it is not stretched.
8. Trim edge with scissors or sharp knife to overlap ½ in. Fold extra pastry under at edge and press edges together with a fork, or flute. Prick bottom and sides of shell thoroughly with a fork. (Omit pricking if filling is to be baked in shell.)
9. Bake at 450°F 10 to 15 min., or until crust is light golden brown. Cool on cooling rack.

*One 8- or 9-in. pastry shell*
*20 min.*

**Pastry Tart Shells:** Follow recipe for Pastry for 1-Crust Pie. Use muffin pan wells, heat resistant custard cups or 3-in. tart pans. Roll pastry ⅛ in. thick and cut about ½ in. larger than over-all size of pans used. Carefully fit rounds into pans without stretching, fold excess pastry under at edge and press together with a fork, or flute. Prick bottom and sides of shells with fork. (Omit pricking if filling is to be baked in shell.) Bake at 450°F 8 to 10 min., or until light golden brown. Cool. Carefully remove tart shells from pans.

*23 min.*

# Pastry Turnovers

Pastry for 1-Crust Pie (on this page)
Mincemeat (If using packaged condensed mincemeat, follow directions on package.)

1. Prepare Pastry for 1-Crust Pie.
2. Roll dough into a rectangle about 1/8 in. thick. Cut into 4-in. squares. Place mincemeat in center of each square.
3. Fold in half diagonally, pressing edges together with floured fork. Prick tops in several places with fork.
4. Bake at 450°F about 15 min., or until turnovers are golden brown.
5. Thick, sweetened applesauce, jam or jelly may be used to fill turnovers.

*7 turnovers*
*25 min.*

# Lazy Man's Coffee Cake

1¾ cup All-in-One Biscuit Mix (page 72)
¼ cup firmly packed brown sugar
½ teaspoon cinnamon
⅓ cup sugar
1 egg
¼ cup milk

1. Grease the bottom of an 8-in. round layer cake pan.
2. For Sugar Topping—Lightly mix ¼ cup all-in-one Biscuit Mix, ¼ cup firmly packed brown sugar and cinnamon.
3. For Coffee Cake—Blend thoroughly 1½ cups all-in-one Biscuit Mix and ⅓ cup sugar.
4. Beat egg until thick and piled softly.
5. Add milk and beat until blended.
6. Add liquid to dry ingredients all at one time; mix only enough to moisten dry ingredients. Turn into pan. Spoon sugar mixture over coffee cake batter.
7. Bake at 375°F about 20 min., or until a cake tester or wooden pick comes out clean when inserted in center of coffee cake.
8. Cut while warm and serve.

*6 servings*
*25 min.*

**Coconut Coffee Cake:** Follow recipe for Lazy Man's Coffee Cake. Substitute the following **Coconut Topping** for the Sugar Topping.
For Coconut Topping—Cream together ⅓ cup **sugar** and 3 tablespoons **butter** or **margarine.** Blend in 2 tablespoons **cream** and ½ teaspoon **cinnamon.** Continue blending until mixture is very soft. Spread over batter; sprinkle with ¾ cup **flaked coconut.**

*25 min.*

# Spice Drops

3 cups All-in-One Biscuit Mix (page 72)
1 cup firmly packed brown sugar
1½ teaspoons cinnamon
½ teaspoon allspice
½ teaspoon nutmeg
¼ teaspoon cloves
2 eggs, well beaten
3 tablespoons milk
1½ teaspoons vanilla extract
¼ teaspoon orange extract

1. Lightly grease cookie sheets.
2. Blend biscuit mix, brown sugar, cinnamon, allspice, nutmeg and cloves in a mixing bowl.
3. Beat eggs, milk, vanilla extract and orange extract until blended.
4. Make a well in center of dry ingredients and add liquid mixture all at one time. Beat until batter is smooth. Carefully scrape around sides and bottom of bowl several times during mixing. Drop dough by teaspoonfuls about 2 in. apart onto cookie sheets.
5. Bake at 375°F about 10 min., or until delicately browned.

*About 5½ doz. cookies*
*30 min.*

**Oatmeal Drops:** Follow recipe for Spice Drops. Omit orange extract and spices except for cinnamon. When batter is smooth, stir in ½ cup uncooked **rolled oats,** ½ cup (about 2 oz.) chopped **nuts** and ½ cup **flaked coconut.**

*30 min.*

**Peanut Butter Checks:**  Follow recipe for Spice Drops. Cut ⅓ cup softened **peanut butter** into mix. Substitute **granulated sugar** for brown. Omit spices and orange extract. Flatten cookies with floured fork by making crisscross marks on top.

*30 Min.*

**Chocolate Drops:** Follow recipe for Spice Drops. Melt and cool 1 sq. (1 oz.) **chocolate.** Substitute **granulated sugar** for brown. Omit spices and orange extract. When batter is smooth, blend in melted chocolate. Press a **walnut** half onto each cookie.

*30 min.*

**Semi-Sweet Drops:** Follow recipe for Spice Drops. Omit spices and orange extract. Blend in 1 pkg. (6 oz.) **semi-sweet chocolate pieces** and ½ cup (about 2 oz.) chopped **nuts.**

*30 min.*

**Gumdrop Chews:** Follow recipe for Spice Drops. Omit spices. Blend in 1½ cups chopped **gumdrops** (do not use licorice-flavored gumdrops.)

*30 min.*

# INDEX